Q & A
for Every Day

Insights:

The Wisdom
and
Compassion
of a
Buddhist Master

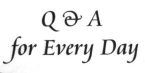

Q & A
for Every Day

Insights:

The Wisdom
and
Compassion
of a
Buddhist Master

By Venerable Master Hsuan Hua

Translated and Published by
Buddhist Text Translation Society
Dharma Realm Buddhist University
Dharma Realm Buddhist Association

Q & A for Every Day

Insights: The Wisdom and Compassion of a Buddhist Master

Questions & Answers given in Chinese

Translated into English by the

Buddhist Text Translation Society

Compilation by Upasika Liu Guo Jie

Review of Compilation by

Bhikshunis Heng Syin Shi and Jin Fu Shi

Translation by Bhikshuni Jin Gwang Shi

Edited by Bhikshuni Jin Rou Shi, Bill and Maureen Dorey

Editorial assistance by Ukasika Soohoong Leong

Publication Editor: Heng Lung Shi

Layout and Graphics by

Upasaka Roger Chiong,

Upasikas Hean and Seng Chang

English translation certified by Bhikshuni Heng Chih Shi

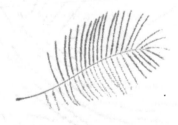

Q & A for Every Day
Insights: The Wisdom and Compassion of a Buddhist Master

1st English edition
Copyright @ 2008 by
Buddhist Text Translation Society
Dharma Realm Buddhist University
Dharma Realm Buddhist Association

ISBN 978-1-60103-001-6
Published by
Buddhist Text Translation Society
4951 Bodhi Way
Ukiah, California 95482

Printed in Malaysia

Library of Congress Cataloging-in-Publication Data

Hsüan Hua, 1908-
   [Jin gang bang he. English]
   Insights : the wisdom and compassion of a Buddhist Master :
Q & A for every day / Hsuan Hua. -- 1st Eng. ed.
      p. cm.
   ISBN 978-1-60103-001-6 (hard bound : alk. paper)
1. Religious life--Buddhism. I. Title.

   BQ5410.H77513 2007
   294.3'444--dc22

                                                2007011469

The Eight Guidelines of
The Buddhist Text Translation Society

1. A volunteer must free him/herself from the motives of personal fame and profit.
2. A volunteer must cultivate a respectful and sincere attitude free from arrogance and conceit.
3. A volunteer must refrain from aggrandizing his/her work and denigrating that of others.
4. A volunteer must not establish him/herself as the standard of correctness and suppress the work of others with his or her fault-finding.
5. A volunteer must take the Buddha-mind as his/her own mind.
6. A volunteer must use the wisdom of Dharma-Selecting Vision to determine true principles.
7. A volunteer must request Virtuous Elders in the ten directions to certify his/her translations.
8. A volunteer must endeavor to propagate the teachings by printing Sutras, Shastra texts, and Vinaya texts when the translations are certified as being correct.

Table of Contents

The City of Ten Thousand Buddhas

*T*he myriad dharmas return to one.

Deep Valley* hears Brahma sounds

As sentient beings leave suffering

And attain Proper Enlightenment.

A thousand doors are non-dual.

Lofty peaks arouse us from confused dreams

As even those without affinities

Receive rescue and certify to Bodhi.

*Ukiah Valley

By Venerable Master Hsuan Hua

Preface

The ways in which the Venerable Master taught his disciples certainly were ultimate expedients, both wholesome and astute. Sometimes he used a tap and a shout, sometimes, an opportune poke. Sometimes he showed repeated kindness, as a mother would. Sometimes he scolded sharply, as a stern father might. In general, he was able to directly reach sentient beings with varying faculties and particular causes and conditions by offering teachings according to their propensities.

We disciples, in receiving the Master's personal guidance, profoundly cherish and remember his teaching that regarded all beings with great kindness and recognized their fundamental identity.

Virtually all of us disciples have had the same experience of being apart from the Master and yet having his teaching right with us as a shadow follows a form.

And so it happens that when we awaken in the morning wondering about something, we receive an answer that day at lunch on the audio recording of the Master, aired totally without any plan or contrivance. Or we have some idle thought during the day and that evening while listening to an audio recording of the Master, he reveals our false thinking without the least politeness. It is impossible to count the number of times his teaching, in such inconceivable ways, has reached us over the decades of the Master-disciple relationship.

Even now, although the Master is no longer physically present, still his teaching continues just as always.

Lunar fifth month 10th day, 2001
6th memorial of the Venerable Master's Nirvana

Venerable Master Hsuan Hua

Biography of
Master Hsuan Hua

The Venerable Master Hsuan Hua was also known as An Tse and To Lun. The name Hsuan Hua was bestowed upon him after he received the transmission of the Wei Yang Lineage of the Chan School from Venerable Elder Hsu Yun. Venerable Master Hua was born in Manchuria in 1918. He left the home life at the age of nineteen. After the death of his mother, he lived in a tiny thatched hut by her graveside for three years, as an act of filial respect. During that time, he practiced meditation and studied the Buddha's teachings. Among his many practices were eating only once a day at midday and never lying down to sleep.

He cultivated various practices of purity and traveled to study with various eminent and virtu-ous monks, such as the Venerable Elder Hsu Yun. In 1948 the Master arrived in Hong Kong, where he founded the Buddhist Lecture Hall and other monasteries. In 1962 he brought the Proper Dharma to America and the West, where he lectured extensively on the major works of the Mahayana Buddhist canon. Delivering more than ten thousand lectures, he was the first person to establish the Triple Jewel in the United States. Over the years, the Master established the Dharma Realm Buddhist Association (DRBA) and its numerous affiliated monasteries and centers. He taught both Western and Asian disciples to apply the Dharma in daily life. He also taught disciples to translate the canon and set up educational institutions, and he guided the Sangha members in DRBA monasteries to truly practice and uphold the Buddhadharma.

The Master passed into stillness on June 7, 1995, in Los Angeles, U.S.A., causing many people throughout the world to mourn the sudden setting of the sun of wisdom. Although he has passed on, his lofty example will always be remembered. Throughout his life he worked selflessly and vigorously to benefit the people of the world and all living beings.

His wisdom and compassion inspired many to correct their faults and lead wholesome lives. Here we include the Verse of the Mendicant of Chang Bai written by the Venerable Master to serve as a model for all of us to emulate.

The Mendicant of Chang Bai was simple
and honest in nature.
He always wished to help and benefit people.
Forgetting himself for the sake of the Dharma,
he was willing to sacrifice his life.
Bestowing medicines according to illnesses,
he offered his own flesh and bones.
His vow: to unite as one with millions of beings.
His practice: to pervade space as he gathers in
vast numbers of those with different potentials,
without regard for past, future, or present, and
with no distinctions of north, south, east, or west.

The Master (Shr Fu)

Master:

Let me first make this clear: I won't answer difficult questions because I don't have a great deal of wisdom. I also won't answer simple questions because I will be wasting other people's time.

Q: Master, will you please tell us your life experiences?

A: My experience has been to do no business. That's my experience.

ဆ၁က

Q: In your poem, "White Universe," there is a phrase, "One breaks the cover of empty space with two fists." What does it mean?

A: There is no meaning to it. If it meant anything, the cover of empty space would not be broken.

ဆ၁က

Q: The Master always says "To truly recognize our faults and do not discuss the faults of others. Others' fault are simply my own. That is great compassion." However, the Venerable Master often criticizes others (in the Vajra Bodhi Sea). Doesn't that mean you don't practice what you preach?

A: If what I say is true, then I'm not finding fault with them; if what I say were false, then I would go to hell. You know the person who said, "Great cultivators are not affected by cause and effect," had to face the consequence of being a fox for 500 lives. I would go to the tongue-pulling hell if I were wrong or have twisted the facts by treating black as white, white as black, true as false, and false as true. If what I say is correct, I am not guilty. Why do I talk about the ways in which others are right or wrong? It is because there is too much gossip in the Buddhist community, calling this one the Black Sect, that one the White Sect, Yellow Sect, Red Sect. There are so many colors that they blind people's ability to tell them apart. They can't tell that black is black and white is white. Therefore, I must say what others dare not say.

ༀ☯ༀ

Q: Master, would you please beat me over the head a few more times?

A: Don't be greedy.

Q: Master, which Dharma Master do you most respect in this lifetime?

A: Venerable Master Hsu Yun.

80C3

Q: Master, please be compassionate and save my daughter. She was diagnosed with hereditary weak metabolism, which has affected her bones and heart.

A: When I was in Hong Kong, there was a five-year-old child who couldn't walk. His mother brought him to bow to the Buddhas at our monastery in the mountains every day. After half a year, he was well without having to take any medication. Please ask the person who bowed to the Buddhas. I don't understand it.

Q & A - *Shr Fu*
5

ಬಿಡಿ

Q: Master, I have heard you call yourself stupid on many occasions. You are probably being humble. However, if you say that too often, it may reflect your lack of self-confidence and indecisiveness. How could you preside over an organization that way? And what exactly does stupidity mean?

A: If I were not stupid, why would I tell the mosquitoes to bite me instead of other people? If I were not stupid, why wouldn't I be interested in more money? If I were not stupid, why would I renounce what most people find enjoyable? What else do you call this but stupidity?

ಬಿಡಿ

Q: Master, since you still reminisce about China, why did you establish your monasteries in the United States?

A: I have always been the one to take what others have abandoned and to go where others don't want to go. There are plenty of temples in Taiwan already.

ഇഇ

Q: Most people say that you have several kinds of supernatural powers?

A: I will not admit to it. It's just coincidental. Those who are meant to live will not die by asking me for help. Those who are meant to die will not live by asking me for help. Do you understand?

ഇഇ

Q: Venerable Master, since becoming a monk, you have persevered in maintaining a life according to the precepts such as "eating one meal a day" and "sleeping sitting up." Is it necessary for you to suffer so much?

A: I want to save my food and my clothes for other living beings. I made this vow: may I bear the sufferings of all living beings in the Dharma Realm.

ଽୠଔ

Q: Master, are you tired?

A: I might as well die from fatigue.

ଽୠଔ

Q: Please tell us where the Dharma Master will be going after your death?

A: There is nowhere to go.

ଽୠଔ

Q: Master, how do we say thank you at the City of Ten Thousand Buddhas?

A: People at the City of Ten Thousand Buddhas do not say thank you. Whoever says so will be fined $500. I never say these two words, "thank you." That's why rumor has it that I only like to yell at people.

ଽୠଔ

Q: Master, in your Dharma talks, you told us to study Chan samadhi. We really want to learn, but you will be going back to the U.S. shortly. We will not have an opportunity to learn from you.

A: If you have enough faith, I can teach you every day, not only while in Taiwan, but from the U.S. also.

૪૦૯૪

Q: Someone says that so-and-so is a devil and that he should be kicked out.

A: It's precisely because he's so awful that I'm trying to teach and transform him. I'll leave the good people for that "someone" to convert.

૪૦૯૪

Q: What are the qualifications to becoming your disciples?

A: You must change yourself.

૪૦૯૪

Q: I have heard many people say that culti-vators are protected by many gods, dragons, and Dharma protectors. Cultivators have many mystical experiences. May I ask the Master what kind of mystical experiences or miracles have you encountered?

A: I have encountered many miracles, but I don't know about the eightfold heavenly dragons, ninefold earth dragons, or tenfold human dragons.

৪০৫

Q: It just so happens that the third week of next month will be the Master's birthday. Would you allow us to hold a birthday celebra-tion for you?

A: You could celebrate my birthday by reciting the names of Earth Store Bodhisattva and Guan-shiyin Bodhisattva 10,000 times every day. Can you do it? This would be a real birthday celebration. Birthdays are better left to the gods than to people.

Q: Can bows made on a bowing pilgrimage be counted toward the 10,000 bows that we must do? (Editor's note: The Venerable Master required that anyone who takes refuge with him must bow 10,000 times)

A: I asked you to bow 10,000 times for taking refuge with the Triple Jewel, but you try to negotiate and pull numbers from here and there. This is not a business and you are not paying off a loan. If you can't complete the bows, you are not sincere enough. We are not bargaining over prices.

⌘

Q: What are your vows?

A: Buddhism in China is generally conservative. I want Buddhist Sutras to be translated into English. Why are Catholicism and Christianity so prevalent? It is because they have translated the Bible into different languages. Buddhists should translate the Sutras into different languages, taking their cue from Catholics and Christians. I am ready to integrate every religion at the City of Ten Thousand Buddhas. Every religion may conduct their services in the new facilities we plan to build. By being inclusive, I believe sectarian thinking will diminish.

ॐ

Q: At Chang Geng Hospital in Linko (Taiwan), I saw the Master beat a patient over the head with your cane. What was that supposed to mean?

A: I did not like the looks of that sick patient, so I hit him.

ॐ

Q: If no one were to make any donations, where would you get food to sustain you?

A: In that case, I might as well starve to death.

ဆာလ

Q: Master, what is your view on spiritual penetrations? Do you have any?

A: What spiritual penetrations? I don't even have ghostly penetrations, let alone spiritual ones. I don't talk about spiritual penetration, only wisdom. Intuition or foresight could be a result of your wisdom, not necessarily because of spiritual penetration. Our spirit has incredible power. If you behave properly and follow the rules, you will naturally have that wisdom after some time. Spiritual penetrations are some minor abilities developed on our spiritual path. They are not worth mentioning. Don't think they are something special. People who really cultivate do not pay attention to them and do not reject them either. They are a natural tendency.

ဆာလ

Q: Please describe the spirit of Venerable Master Hsu Yun.

A: He did not sleep.

ಬಂಞ

Q: Master, what motivated you to become a monk in the first place?

A: Why do you want to know about my becoming a monk? You want to dig into my roots that are long gone.

ಬಂಞ

Q: Master, why do you always walk behind your disciples?

A: I pick up what people toss away. I let people have what they want. To pick up what people toss away is to not fight, to not be greedy, and to not seek. To let people have what they want is to be selfless, to refrain from pursuing personal advantage, and to refrain from lying.

※※※

Q: I would like to make some offerings to you, but I don't know what to give.

A: The best offering to me is the recitation of the Buddha's name. To recite the Buddha's name sincerely is an offering of sincerity; to recite the Buddha's name with a commitment to precepts is an offering of commitment to the precepts; to recite the Buddha's name with samadhi is an offering of samadhi; to recite the Buddha's name with wisdom is an offering of wisdom.

※※※

Q: We respectfully request the compassionate Master to save the patients who have passed away in this hospital so that they may avoid suffering.

A: I already reflected on that as I came in. I have already dedicated merit and virtue to those who died though they shouldn't have, and those who cannot transcend their current realm. Nothing that I do has to be visible.

∞◌∞

Q: My second question is, why is your Dharma name Hsuan Hua?

A: Why do you want to know about my name? This is a ghost from hells!

∞◌∞

Q: The City of Ten Thousand Buddhas is too big!

A: The City is not too big. Your mind is too small.

∞◌∞

Q: I want to donate a monastery to be one of your branch temples in Taiwan. Would you like to have it, Master?

A: You have to ask yourself. Don't ask me. If I were to say that I want it, then I must be greedy. If I were to say that I don't want it, then I would not be granting your vow to make this donation. You have wisdom, so you should decide for yourself. It's up to you whether you make the donation or not.

ಬಂಡ

Q: Has the Master been sick before? If so, how did you treat yourself? Did you heal yourself or did you use Western medicine?

A: "Sickness enters through the mouth, disasters exit out of the mouth." You'll get sick if you eat good food that is too nourishing. I don't dare to eat anything good, that's why I don't get sick. I don't have money to use Western medicine, and even less money to take Chinese medicine. So I figure that I might as well not use any doctor. It's okay to die and it's okay to live.

ಬಂಡ

Q *Reporter*: Why did the Dharma Master think about coming westward to North America to propagate the Buddhadharma?

A: Buddhism wasn't growing in America several decades back. Some places here have never heard of Buddhism. That's why I had decided to come and propagate Buddhism in a country without it. I do what I must do regardless of whether people accept it or not.

☙◊❧

Q: If I were to give my afflictions to you, what would I be left with?

A: Wouldn't it be better if you were to have no more afflictions while I did? I can handle them.

☙◊❧

Q: Some people say that you are an old demon king. What should we do about that?

A: So I am the old demon king!

ဝဝ

Q: My child took refuge with the Master when he was three or so. What happens if he can't finish bowing his ten thousand bows?

A: There are lots of young people in America who took refuge with me when they were still in their mothers' womb. What do you think they should do?

ဝဝ

Q: Master, did you make every one of the ten thousand Buddhas in the Buddha Hall of the City of Ten Thousand Buddhas!

A: It's all in the past. Why mention it?

ဝဝ

Q: I know that the Master doesn't like to hear people say thank you, but I am grateful to the Master for saving my life on several occasions.

A: Expand your mind, don't be so petty. Hurry up and reflect. Return to your original purity!

೫೦೦೮

Q: Master, if you were to say that you were enlightened, would that mean that you are not enlightened?

A: If I were to say that I am not enlightened, it wouldn't mean that I'm enlightened either. Why do people have to say they are enlightened?

೫೦೦೮

Q: Has the Master seen ghosts before?

A: I will not answer such a question. Why? Because even if I have, you haven't. If I were to say that I haven't, you would still think that I have. So this is a question that shouldn't be answered.

೫೦೦೮

Q: I would like to set up a long life plaque for the Venerable Master.

A: How can I help others if I need other people's help?

೮೮೮

Q: We earnestly request that the Venerable Master remain in the world. (People expressed this on three different occasions in 1990.)

A: I didn't say I was leaving. This kind of thing is predetermined.

೮೮೮

Q: Why does that bird sit in the Master's palm without flying away?

A: Because I have no thought of killing.

೮೮೮

Q: Have you ever smoked cigarettes before?

A: Since you have, it's as if I have.

⁎

Q: Why is the Master's memory so excellent? How should most people develop theirs?

A: Practice to perfection getting rid of outflows in life after life.

⁎

Q: Master, what have been your greatest delights and disappointments in the past?

A: I enjoyed helping people the most. I am most disappointed to have lied: not being able to do what I said I would.

⁎

Q: The Venerable Master always bows five times before and after speaking the Dharma. What's the significance?

A: The first bow is to all Buddhas throughout the ten directions and three periods of time.

The second bow is to the Dharma spoken by all Buddhas throughout the ten directions and three periods of time. The third bow is to holy as well as ordinary members of the Sangha throughout the ten directions and three periods of time. The fourth bow is to all beings throughout the Dharma Realm. The fifth bow is to all the pratimoksha spoken by all Buddhas throughout the ten directions and three periods of time. Each one of the five bows is a bow that reaches all places.

ಶುಲ

Q: How many disciples have taken refuge with you in the United States?

A: I have never counted. And I don't care to either.

ಶುಲ

Q: Great Master, let me first ask you, why did you became a monk?

A: I was probably meant to be a monk.

෨෮෬

Q: The Master hasn't eaten for a week in order to pray for rain. Should we notify the newspapers now that it's raining in both the United States and Taiwan?

A: I fast to transfer merit and virtue to all living beings; it's not for fame. Don't advertise.

Q: Why shouldn't we notify the newspapers about our praying for rain?

A: It doesn't work that way.

෨෮෬

Q: May our kind teacher live forever to propagate the Buddhadharma and universally save all sentient beings.

A: I am already dead.

෨෮෬

Q: Many Buddhists come here to dump their frustrations and problems.

A: I don't know how to teach and transform people, so I am extremely ashamed every day. If I knew how to save people, then all of you would have become free of afflictions a long time ago.

৪০৫৪

Q: Why doesn't the Master wear better clothes and eat better food?

A: If I eat well and dress well, then my disciples will also eat well and dress well. How can we cultivate that way?

৪০৫৪

Q: The car that the Venerable Master uses is small and hot!

A: The hells are even hotter!

৪০৫৪

Q: A certain person you are acquainted with asked another person to bring some donations for the Master.

A: That particular money is meant as a bribe. I will not accept it. Return it immediately.

୨୦୯ଓ

Q: How did the Venerable Master propagate the Buddhadharma in the West?

A: On the power of Guan Shi Yin Bodhisatva, the Great Compassion Mantra, and the Shurangama Mantra.

୨୦୯ଓ

Q: Master, there are many members of the eightfold division, such as dragons, gods, and Dharma protecting good spirits on the sides of the road bowing to the Master.

A: Where do I have the virtue?

₨₧

Q *Member of audience*: This Dharma Master sure likes to insult people. He has to insult people even while lecturing on the Sutras.

A: I didn't insult anyone else. When I insult you, I'm insulting myself. So I insult myself everyday.

₨₧

Q: Master, if you don't eat you will collapse.

A: It's only my body that hurts if I don't eat. However, if you do not cultivate well, my heart is in even more pain.

₨₧

Q: Master, you have been a monk for so many years. Although you've been in the United States, you still think about your homeland. What are you most sad about?

A: I wrote a verse before:

> As I reflect on several decades of
> chaos in China,
> I am overcome with sadness.
> My tears form a pool.
> Unfortunately I do not have the ability
> to turn back fate.
> I cannot use a well-aimed arrow
> to shoot down time that has already passed.
> The ways of the world are crooked and twisted
> by the cunning of humans and ghosts.
> The ups and downs of politics
> appall us all.
> Having not forgotten my loyalty
> despite being a monk,
> I keep my nationality to be faithful
> to my origins.

Do you know what I mean? My country has been chaotic for so many years; the Chinese are too sad! I can't help but shed tears when I think about it. Although being Chinese we experience so much hardship, I still want to preserve my nationality. The Chinese must have moral fiber!

ଊଓ

Q: Why is it that every time we go out, the Master never seems tired, yet the disciples end up being exhausted?

A: It's not that I am not tired, but that I overcome it with my willpower.

ଊଓ

Q: The Venerable Master's cultivation can affect dragons and gods. We suggest that the Venerable Master save all our fellow citizens who have suffered in the last several hundred years.

A: Ghosts and spirits who died several thousand years ago have all arrived here at the Protecting the Nation and Quelling Disasters Guanyin Great Compassion Dharma Assembly. The deceased have been ferried over to the shore of liberation. You just don't know

about it. I know you find what I am saying now
unbelievable.

ॐ

Q: Why do Bodhisattvas when they make
vows use the qualification of not becoming a
Buddha to give power to these vows?

A: Those are not Bodhisattvas; they are
ghosts. Ghosts fall into the three evil paths.
Such beings will not become Buddhas soon.
They are on the slow path. Just like me. That's
why I say I am a ghost. You don't believe me
at all because you see me as being a person. I
saved some ghosts in the past, so they dragged
me into the hells. No one would pull me out
even if I wanted them to. So I chose to stay in
the hells and do what I could. I saw that my
ghost friends were suffering, so I thought I
would wait until they became Buddhas before
I became a Buddha. However, my vow cannot
compare with that of Earth Store Bodhisattva's
vow of not becoming a Buddha until the hells

are empty. For me, if there's even a single ghost, I will not become a Buddha. The hells may not necessarily be empty because I'm talking about ghosts in the present time. I will not bother with those in the future. There will be another time for that.

ಐಅಂ

Q: Why does the Venerable Master want to go into seclusion when you have not yet recovered physically?

A: I have to go into seclusion for a month for the war in Iraq. I want to help by dedicating merit and virtue to the locals there.

ಐಅಂ

Q: Why is the Master wearing a green bracelet all of sudden?

A: A spirit from several millenniums ago is still possessive when it comes to this bracelet. It'll be a while before she can let go of it and become liberated.

༄༅

Q: Does the Master want to do some sightseeing?

A: Sightseeing? I've seen everything.

༄༅

Q: Natural disasters are occurring often recently, will the Master please not go to Taiwan.

A: If I deserve this retribution, then I'll accept it.

༄༅

A visitor was shooting pictures of the Venerable Master left and right, wanting lots of photos.

Master: Don't take so many pictures. You shouldn't be so greedy. Just take one picture, don't take too many! You're not the only one eating. Be content. The Dharma is impartial and not hierarchical. Don't be eager for too much of anything; you'll only bite off more than you can chew.

ഇൽ

Q: Were you talking about causes and conditions from past lives when you mentioned earlier how people have seen you in the past?

A: Possibly, who knows?

ഇൽ

Q: Is it the case that all disciples who have taken refuge with the Venerable Master, whether monastic or lay, will be able to avoid transmigration in the six destinies?

A: Those who have taken refuge with me, but who are unruly, doing all kinds of bad things, cannot avoid transmigration in the six destinies. Those who have not taken refuge with me but try their best to do good deeds can also avoid transmigration in the six destinies.

ഇൽ

Q: Many people are unhappy with what the Master said; but there are lots of people who are happy too.

A: The purpose of my saying things is not to make people happy or unhappy. I just say what is true and what accords with the principles of truth. That's what I have always known to do.

߷

Q: Why do some people have dreams about the Master even before they meet you? Is it that they have affinities with you from the past? Or is it that the Venerable Master emits light that makes people dream about you?

A: I don't have that much light, that much gasoline. Cause and effect is the reason. People have affinities with others. Those who have deeper affinities with others will recall impressions from their past. These past affinities unveil themselves of their own accord. Many people are delighted to see me, especially children, who will do everything that I tell them. In Northeast China, without being told, some teenagers used to prostrate, bow, and do all kinds of things when they first saw me. Some people cry when they see me; some are ecstatic. When asked why they cry, they say they feel like children who have been lost from their parents for a long time. They feel as if they have finally come home after years of suffering. They release their pent-up angst and have a good cry when they know they've come home. There are many, many different situations, but I don't want to tell you about them. If I were to tell you, you all would cry too.

Q: Master, why don't you have any attendants?

A: I really can't help it! If my attendants were Chinese, then my American disciples would be unhappy. If my attendants were Americans, then my Chinese disciples would be unhappy. If my attendants were male, my female disciples would be unhappy. If my attendants were female, then my male disciples would be unhappy. If my attendants were young, then the older ones would be unhappy.

୨୦୯୨

Q: Master, you said that you started to bow to all living beings since the age of twelve. Is this a vow from your lives past and you have returned to this world again for this lifetime?

A: I can't prove this, so I can't respond.

୨୦୯୨

Q: Will the Venerable Master please be kind and compassionate and ease the suffering of the Chinese?

A: That is a vow of mine. I am willing to take

on the suffering of every Chinese and I dedicate
to them all the blessings that are meant for me.

৪০৫৪

Q: They say you're really mean, you yell at
people.

A: Not only do I yell at people, I hit them!

৪০৫৪

*A sincere Catholic didn't know what to do
when he first stepped into the Buddha Hall as
a guest.*

*Suddenly the Venerable Master appeared and
said with much kindness: Just treat this like your
home. Do what you think is right. Don't worry.
The guest became relaxed.*

৪০৫৪

Q: To what religious school do you belong?

A: The one-meal-a-day school.

୫୬୯ଓ

Q: From which part of China did you come? How did you begin learning about the Buddhadharma?

A: I probably could not finish my answer to this question in several years. To put it simply, I enjoyed learning the Buddhadharma so I studied the Buddhadharma. I am originally from China, but I believe that I'm not Chinese, American, or Japanese. (No country wants me because I am a dummy.) I didn't come down from Heaven. I'm no Jesus. I didn't come from the Land of Ultimate Bliss, so I'm not Amitabha Buddha. I'm not from the Land of Lapis Lazuli, so I'm not Medicine Master Buddha who Quells Disasters and Lengthens Life.

୫୬୯ଓ

Q: I want to donate a large Buddha statue for the Great Heroes Jeweled Hall, is this okay?

A: Okay, but hurry. Otherwise it will be gone.

That disciple didn't understand why he should hurry. The Great Heroes Jeweled Hall hasn't even been built yet. Could it be that someone will grab the opportunity to donate before him? That couldn't be yet. He thought he might as well go and invest that money. Wouldn't it be better to earn more money in the next couple of years and donate two large Buddha statues? In the end, the investment was completely awash because his partners swindled the entire amount. Only then did he realize that what the Venerable Master meant by "it will be gone." He meant the money would be gone.

જીલ્સ

Q: Master, you get so many letters every day. Do you collect the stamps on the envelopes? They'll become valuable later on.

A: I don't want money.

ೲಢ

Q: Master, why don't you live in a warmer room or turn on the heater to keep warm?

A: I like being in an ice box.

ೲಢ

A disciple's older sister came to the City of Ten Thousand Buddhas for the first time and met the Venerable Master. Venerable Master: Yu Bin is a good friend of mine.

That disciple didn't understand why the Master would talk about Cardinal Yu Bin with his sister all of a sudden. After the Venerable Master left, the disciple's sister said: Strange, I was able to come to the United States to attend college because I received the Yu Bin Scholarship after graduating from Taipei's Number One Girls High School. You didn't even know that, how did the Venerable Master know?

ೲಢ

Q: Will the Master please bless everybody?

A: I did it a long time ago, you just didn't know about it.

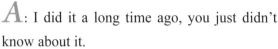

Venerable Master: There's good and bad in everything.

Visitor: So there's no difference between good and evil.

Venerable Master: That type of viewpoint is deviant.

Visitor: I believe the Master is out of time.

Venerable Master: My time stretches into the end of time throughout the future.

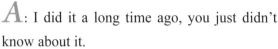

Q: Master has eyes in his palm!

A: Not just in my palm, they're in every pore.

☞☜

Q: Why does the Venerable Master know so many things?

A: When I want to know, I know everything. When I don't want to know, I know nothing.

☞☜

Q: What does the Venerable Master think of hierarchy?

A: All living beings are family members; the universe makes up my body; emptiness is my university. My name is nonexistent, and I practice kindness, compassion, joy, and equanimity.

Disciples

Q: As your disciple, how do I cultivate wisdom?

A: You can cultivate wisdom by not being deluded. You become wise once you throw away your delusions. Your Dharma-nature appears when you see through ignorance. It's as easy as flipping your hand.

ଥ୦ଓ

Q: Master, before you came here last year, I dreamed of at least seven Honored Ones wearing red precept sashes and hats embroidered with the images of five Buddhas descending from the heavens. Even though I have dreamed of Buddha and Bodhisattvas before, I had never dreamed of so many at one time. Please kindly accept my sincere bow and give me your explanation.

A: Since you know about wearing the hat with the images of Buddhas, why don't you wear it now?

ଥ୦ଓ

Q: Your disciples in the Gaoshong area really need your guidance. May we ask the Venerable Master to build a monastery at Gaoshong?

A: I do not have the capability to build a monastery. If anyone of you will be building a monastery, I can be a construction worker.

ဆၣ

Q: Does everyone have the affinity to become your disciple?

A: You have the affinity if you are sincere. Affinity will become no affinity if you're insincere. No affinity will become affinity if you're sincere.

ဆၣ

Q: What health condition is ill-suited for bowing to the Buddhas?

A: All animals and hungry ghosts are suited to bow to the Buddhas. I don't know what kind of condition you have.

ဆၣ

Q: What can we say to show respect?

A: You don't need to say anything, just do it.

೮೮೮

Q: The Youth Good Wealth visited 53 different teachers, so why can't I have a few more masters?

A: The Youth Good Wealth's teachers personally sent him off to his next teacher. He didn't disobey his previous teacher and sneak off to take refuge with other virtuous Dharma Masters whom he had been admiring.

೮೮೮

Q: What are some guiding principles for our Dharma-propagation delegation?

A: Do not accept invitations to meals or banquets. Starve if there are no offerings. You have to suffer when you go out with me. Don't bother with any personal business because this tour is for a country.

ഇന്റെ

Q: We must bow to the Buddhas 10,000 times to take refuge with the Venerable Master. Must we finish those 10,000 bows before we take refuge or is it okay to do the 10,000 bows over time after we have taken refuge?

A: You can do 10,000 bows gradually after taking refuge. After you finish 10,000, you can bow 100,000 or 1,000,000 more. There's no limit.

ഇന്റെ

Q: Buddhism talks about affinities. The Buddha doesn't save anyone with whom he has no affinities. Is it that most people who have no affinities with him just drift along and continue to be lost in the six paths of transmigration? Or can they just learn bits and pieces from the books by the Good Man in the Mill?

A: What kind of books are those? Ask your

question bluntly and directly. There's no need to write an essay on it. "Just because you can string a bunch of words together, that doesn't make you a scholar."

ಶೋಆ

Q: My parents have been dead for many years and I have participated in crossing over ceremonies many times as their son. May I know if my parents have been crossed over to the other shore and in which destiny have they become reborn?

A: Ask somebody who knows. I'm somebody who doesn't know. I can't answer this question of yours. I don't have that kind of knowledge.

ಶೋಆ

Q: Please explain, "One's character is naturally noble when he seeks nothing. All the victories that have been won since ancient times happened solely because of patience."

A: Don't expect anything from people. Patience means that one bears what one cannot bear. However, a master cannot be completely tolerant of his disciples, he has to use both kindness and strength. He spoils his disciple by being too patient with them.

৪৩৬৪

Q: Will you be our master once we leave the householder's life? —

A: I'm already your master without you having to ask! If you think I can be your master, then I'm your master even if you don't ask. However, if you don't cultivate, I'm not your teacher even if you ask.

৪৩৬৪

Q: Are you my teacher from lives past?

A: If you believe, why do you ask? If you ask, it means you doubt.

৪৩৬৪

Q: The Venerable Master says that if we eat too much, we cannot develop our wisdom. So why is one of the Buddhas so chubby and has a big stomach?

A: I've never seen the Buddha. I don't know.

ಯೋಲ್ಡ

Q: I'm really scared that the Master will scold me.

A: Have I ever scolded you before?

Q: Not yet.

A: If anybody scolds you, you should laugh.

ಯೋಲ್ಡ

Q: Master, so and so will be leaving the City of Ten Thousand Buddhas.

A: We don't try to keep people even if they are Bodhisattvas.

ಯೋಲ್ಡ

Q: The Master arrived earlier today because of the way I drove you back to the City of Ten Thousand Buddhas.

A: Don't drive too fast. Don't be too fast or too slow in everything that you do, and then you will be in accord with the Middle Way.

୨୦୯୫

Q: My power of concentration is poor.

A: You haven't any to speak of.

୨୦୯୫

Q: 1. We must bow ten thousand times to the Buddhas to take refuge with the Master. Do we have to recite the repentance text when we bow to the Buddhas? Is it okay that we only bow and not recite sometimes?

2. When I met the Master in 1988, I actually sobbed uncontrollably. What is the reason for that?

3. May I ask about the possibility of my leaving the householder's life?

A: 1. Bowing to the Buddhas is about getting rid of your arrogance. It's also a form of exercise that makes you physically healthy. It's the best way to prevent you from taking too much medication.

2. You were probably hit.

3. As long as you do not kill, steal, commit sexual misconduct, lie, drink alcohol, and take drugs.

❧❦

Q: How long should we wait until someone has been dead before we can cremate the corpse?

A: I've never died before, I wouldn't know how long to wait.

❧❦

Q: When I first joined the profession of nursing, I had compassion, plenty of forgiveness, and diligence that never quit just as I did when I first got a taste of the Buddhadharma. But once I truly and deeply entered nursing, I had feelings about sickness and suffering that could not be resolved. That refreshing feeling for the Buddhadharma also disappeared for me, which became a frustrating quandary that sat in my heart. I'm too weak to be able to comfort living beings completely. I don't seem relieved by reciting the Buddha's name either. What is this all about?

A: Don't be a clay Bodhisattva [who takes on more than he/she can handle].

ཨོཾ

Q: If one of your disciples were to make the great vows of Earth Treasury King Bodhisattva, would that delay the Master's realization of Buddhahood?

A: What does this have to do with you that you need to ask?

ཨོཾ

By a reporter: The Chinese Americans in San Francisco all know that those at the City of Ten Thousand Buddhas are a bunch...

A: Were you about to say "freaks"?

Reporter: No. They say that this is a place for Buddhas; it's where a bunch of monks and nuns practice asceticism (literally "practices of sufferings" in Chinese).

A: We don't suffer at all; conversely, we're doing quite well.

ഇൻയ

Q: Lots of endowments are required for you to have founded so many monasteries and schools. What kind of begging did you do?

A: Beg? I will starve to death before I beg. Consider that when I first arrived in the United States, most people did not understand Buddhism at all. If I were to have gone on alms rounds from door to door, people would have been scared off before they knew anything about Buddhism! So our monks here never beg. People have to come looking for us.

ಬಿಂಡ

Q: Master, I really admire you.

A: Who admires?

ಬಿಂಡ

Q: What principles should we use to guide us when we build the Great Heroes Jeweled Hall in the future?

A: Conserve labor. Easy maintenance.

ಬಿಂಡ

Q: Master, the other car traveling with us is going the wrong way, so I'm going to follow him down the wrong road too.

A: You can't follow him and go wrong just because he has!

ಬಿಂಡ

Q: I would like to start an association to attract more members.

A: I as the teacher have to be responsible for the effect of the mistaken causes that my disciples have sown. You would also have to face the effect of the mistaken causes that you have sown. Don't ever violate the law of cause and effect if you want to cultivate. Don't be greedy.

Q: If the Master doesn't agree that I should establish a certain association, then could we get more people to come and make donations?

A: If monastics can just keep the precepts and cultivate, people will naturally make donations.

ଝୠ

Q: I am really upset! Somebody criticized the Master!

A: Did you thank him for me? How can we cultivate if we can't even let go of that ego?

Q: Why doesn't the Master allow us to notify the newspapers about your donations to various agencies? That way everyone will know that the City of Ten Thousand Buddhas also makes contributions frequently.

A: Do cultivators still pursue fame?

ଈଓଔ

Q: How should disciples cultivate once the Master leaves?

A: Follow the Six Great Guiding Principle. Don't forget the traditions of the City of Ten Thousand Buddhas. Don't try to take advantage of others by developing relationships with them.

ଈଓଔ

Q: The world is a mess right now. In every corner, either a natural or man-made disaster is occurring. Those victims are so sad!

A: How can you be concerned about the world when you haven't done what is right yourself?

∞∞

Q: Master, may I leave the householder's life?

A: There wouldn't be too many with you; there wouldn't be too few without you.

∞∞

Q: What is an arhat? What is the Venerable Master?

A: It's impossible for an elementary school student to know the book that a Ph.D. is reading!

∞∞

Q: What does it mean to make vows? Why should we make vows? How do we make vows?

A: If you want to make vows then you make them. If you don't want to, then don't. Why ask me?

∞∞

Q: Is the accumulation of hidden virtue in the worldly sense the same as "merit and virtue"? Is merit and virtue related to the so-called "good deed"? Is there really merit and virtue in the human realm?

A: If you were to deny cause and effect, then you wouldn't need to believe in anything.

છાজ

Q: Why is there a registration fee for the precepts for the deceased? What should we do if we don't have any money?

A: Why do you have to eat every day? You don't have to receive the precepts for the deceased; nobody is forcing you.

છાજ

Q: Why couldn't this disciple have met the Master earlier in life?

A: Because you didn't make big vows in your past lives.

ಬಂಞ

Q: Master, how did you teach your disciples?

A: I'm interested in education, wishing to nurture the next generation and teach young people and children how to be good people. Both adults and children nowadays don't know how to be people, so they have made our society become disorderly. It's painful to watch.

ಬಂಞ

Q: Many visitors to the City of Ten Thousand Buddhas feel that this place is cold, in the sense of being inhumane.

A: There's no need for social chatter in a monastery, but we don't need to be as cold as ice either.

ಬಂಞ

Q: Venerable Master, I have finally decided to never play the guitar. I want to give it to the Master.

A: If you have really decided to not play, why do you keep it around?

೫೦೪

Q: What kind of attitude should we have to repent and bow the ten thousand bows after we take refuge?

A: Be without a mind. No mental attitude. Don't think about anything.

೫೦೪

Q: Could I become enlightened?

A: Are you scared to die?

೫೦೪

Q: Could this disciple help?

A: You want to run before you even know how to walk. It's too soon.

ຮດເຊ

Q: Am I enlightened?

A: Do you still have sexual desire?

ຮດເຊ

Q: I remember once when the Venerable Master was giving a Sutra lecture upstairs, you said a certain Dharma Master gave money to people.

A: You remember things very clearly.

ຮດເຊ

Once in a car ride from San Francisco to Gold Wheel Monastery, [Los Angeles,] a disciple was looking at the scenery and telling the

Master how pretty it was there and how nice it was here.

A: I don't look to the outside.

જ⅋જ

Q: Many people teach their disciples mudras to earn more money. Is that a legitimate practice?

A: To do that is to exploit people's greed. Just because they practice mudras, it doesn't mean that all of them will have the power to make every business transaction a success.

જ⅋જ

Q: Somebody said that the Venerable Master has already gone.

A: He's revealing to you how his level of cultivation is beyond that of others!

જ⅋જ

Q: The Master often instructs us that we must accept no remuneration for using the Buddhadharma to heal people, but is meals at a restaurant okay?

A: That is also a form of greed. My true disciples take advantage of no one.

ಬಂದ

Venerable Master: How do we propagate the Buddhadharma in the United States?

Disciple: To end greed, anger, and delusion. To diligently cultivate precepts, samadhi, and wisdom.

Venerable Master: Elaborate. That's too vague.

Disciple: To not fight, not be greedy, not seek, not be selfish, not pursue self-benefit, and not lie.

Venerable Master: Right, that's it.

Venerable Master: Tell me, is it better to write with a piece of white chalk or black chalk on the blackboard?

Disciple: White one.

Venerable Master: Should we use a larger or a smaller piece of white chalk?

Disciple: One of average size.

Venerable Master: Who else would say that? Why do you say a piece that's of an average size? Tell us!

Disciple: A large piece breaks easily. A small piece is difficult to handle. We can write with a piece that's medium in size.

Venerable Master: Do you see me with a large piece or small piece every time I write? Or do I use a medium-sized one?

Disciple: A small piece.

Venerable Master: Then I must not write well?

Disciple: No! It's just that the Venerable Master wants to be frugal.

Venerable Master: And what does that mean? It means to cherish and use anything that can still be used. Only when something cannot be used anymore do we stop using it. We do not waste anything.

∞○∞

Venerable Master: Do you know why you've got a hunched back?

Disciple: I don't know.

Venerable Master: Because you're always thinking about other people's reaction to everything that you do.

ৰ০তস

Q: Uh oh, so-and-so is leaving, who is going to be translating in the future?

A: No one is indispensable. It's never the case that only one person can do some thing.

ৰ০তস

A disciple asked an inappropriate question.

A: Gee, you wasted a lot of your gasoline!

ৰ০তস

Q: There's a City of Ten Thousand Buddhas in Canada too! Where is it?

A: At Golden. We can build a Buddhist Village there that comes with monasteries, schools, elders' homes, and creates job opportunities for lay people to settle there while working. You can go there to build the Buddhist Village after you retire.

ஐௐ

Q: The hospital building (at the City of Ten Thousand Buddhas) has many leaks. To renovate the whole thing will require several tens of thousands of dollars.

A: That's too expensive. Just do spot repairs.

ஐௐ

A disciple told the Venerable Master what his job duties were at the time.

V enerable Master: Don't use your authority to oppress people, but move and transform people through personal example.

ஐௐ

V enerable Master: Do you like candy?

A child: I don't like American candy. I only like Chinese candy.

(*The Venerable Master then took out a box of*

hard candy made in Taiwan and gives it to the child.)

T he child couldn't help but utter: This is my favorite candy. Thank you, Master!

❧

Q: It rained heavily yesterday, many of the roofs at the City are leaking.

A: Who told you to have outflows?

❧

Q: Strange, why are there are so many broken pipes at the City of Ten Thousand Buddhas? The water is shooting out too.

A: Who told you to get angry!

❧

Q: Since I decided to become a volunteer at the City of Ten Thousand Buddhas, my professor introduced me to a job that will pay $60,000 in annual salary. The company also offers employee stocks and dividends. Should I take this job?

A: Go ahead if you want to earn money!

The disciple thought about it, "Right, why earn money? Might as well work as a volunteer." *(He decided to move to the City of Ten Thousand Buddhas.)*

ੰੳ

The first time that a disciple visited the City of Ten Thousand Buddhas, he received a phone call from the Master while at the Administrative Office.

The Master blurted out: Everyone at the City of Ten Thousand Buddhas is small.

(That disciple was speechless. It was not until ten years later that that disciple understood how young and righteous he was at the time, extremely arrogant. That's why the Master said

that everyone else was small, to remind the disciple of his egoism.)

ঙ্কষ্ণ

Disciple attending a certain college: I'm in the middle of getting my teaching credential so that I'll have a teaching certificate for being a high school teacher at the conclusion of the program.

A: Your virtue is your certificate for being a teacher. Don't ever attempt homosexuality.

ঙ্কষ্ণ

In 1985, the Venerable Master was training disciples to go up on stage to lecture on the Sutras and give Dharma talks. The Venerable Master only gave a talk and an evaluation at the end.

One newly arrived disciple thought, "I came thousands of miles from Taiwan to the City of Ten Thousand Buddhas just so that I could hear the Venerable Master's Sutra lectures and Dharma talks; but now the Venerable Master isn't speaking. It's so unfair!"

The Venerable Master suddenly walked off the stage and stood next to that disciple, saying, "Who told you not to come earlier?"

ഇൗങ്ങ

Q: I've already taken refuge with the Triple Jewel and have been reciting the Buddha's name diligently and on a regular basis. Why am I still entangled by sicknesses right now?

A: People who have taken refuge with the Triple Jewel still die.

ഇൗങ്ങ

Venerable Master: When you have time in the next few days, cut down that big tree east of the Guest House.

The disciples felt that that large tree was healthy and fine, so they didn't go and cut it down. After a few days, that tree collapsed all of a sudden. Wham, it smashed the roof of the Guest House.

ଈଔଷ

*T*he Venerable Master was going to have his meal at Gold Mountain Monastery. A number of disciples eagerly offered health products and special delicacies to the Master, hoping that he would take them. But the Venerable Master didn't touch any of those items. Then a kid brought an apple over to the Venerable Master.

*V*enerable Master: Is this yours?

*C*hild: Yes.

(That day, the Venerable Master took only that apple for his meal.)

ଈଔଷ

Q: I would like to have my entire family move to the City of Ten Thousand Buddhas and be volunteers. When is a good time to move?

A: The sooner the better.

(That disciple thought three weeks ought to be soon enough because that's summer break for his children. Little would he have guessed that less than a week later his child would be hit by a car on the way home from school. The child lost consciousness and was sent to the emergency room. The accident scared the whole family. Fortunately the child wasn't seriously hurt. As soon as the child was released from the hospital though, the whole family moved. They didn't dare to delay their move any longer.)

ଌଓଔଷ

Q: Why do we rarely see the Venerable Master ride in a car at the City of Ten Thousand Buddhas?

A: Let's not pollute the City's air.

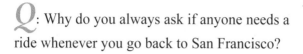

෨෬

Q: Why do you always ask if anyone needs a ride whenever you go back to San Francisco?

A: You don't even understand that? We save a dollar because a carpool of more than three people requires no toll at Golden Gate Bridge. One hundred trips during the year means a savings of $100. You understand now?

෨෬

Venerable Master: Go and look at a piece of land tomorrow.

A disciple: For what should I be looking?

Venerable Master: Make sure that it has mountains, waters, and large trees. You want usable evergreen trees such as pine and cypress. Trees that shed leaves do not make good wood; they're useless. The City of Ten Thousand Buddhas should gradually change its trees that shed to trees such as pine and cypress.

Q: There are some trees at the City of Ten Thousand Buddhas that seem to be withering away and dying gradually. What should we do to save these trees?

A: We don't want those that are withering away and dying. When it's time, they will inevitably die. It's not easy to save something or someone that has lived a long time. Of course we try to save what we can; however, if we can't, we could try nourishing them with the soup from cooking or rinsing rice. If they don't live, we've at least tried our best. All we can do is try our best!

Venerable Master: When there's time, cut down the large tree behind the hospital building.

A disciple: Yes, got it.

When things got busy, that disciple forgot to go and cut down the tree. One month later, one of

the large trees went "boom!" and fell in a wind-
storm. The roof of the hospital was smashed so
that it had a big hole. It was a good thing that
no one was hurt.

৩০০৪

Q: Why don't we put advertisements on television and do some promotions to attract more
people?

A: "Perfume is fragrant on its own, why would
we need a gust to blow it?" We must cultivate
honestly and pay attention to our virtue. Promotions would be useless, too, if we were not
down to earth! We propagate the Dharma and
benefit living beings by lecturing on the Sutras
and giving Dharma talks, not by selling ads.

৩০০৪

Q: Wouldn't the human race become extinct
if everyone were to become a monk or a nun?

A: Could you make everyone become a monk
or a nun?

ഇരുശ

Q: May I become a monk?

A: You are not overly smart, okay.

ഇരുശ

Q: How large is your one meal of the day?

A: It's different depending on whom you talk to. From a child's perspective, I probably eat lot. From an adult perspective, I probably don't eat too much, perhaps a bit less than others. *(To the translator:)* You tell them how much I eat every day.

Translator: Basically a bowl of boiled vegetables. He doesn't eat any oil or salt. He may eat a bowl of rice or some bread, a few pieces of fruit.

Venerable Master: My disciples eat one meal a day. Since I'm their teacher, I should set an even better example. That is why I may skip two or three days between my one meal. It's not for sure.

೫೦೦೮

Venerable Master: Do you know me? Do you know yourself?

A Disciple: I am ashamed...

೫೦೦೮

Q: What responsibilities do we Buddhists of the West have?

A: Your responsibility is to bring Buddhism to the West. Each one of you should make resolutions to contribute yourself to the best of your abilities. Don't rely on others.

೫೦೦೮

Q: I have a dog, I really like...

A: Do you really have to be that intimate with the dog to help it?

☙☯

Venerable Master: Why do we have to die? How can we avoid death?

A relative: The only way to avoid death is to become a monk or nun and cultivate. That's the only way to not die.

☙☯

Once a shramanera (novice monk) was walking around when someone was [performing the ceremony for] requesting Dharma at Gold Mountain Monastery. After the request concluded.

Venerable Master: What are you doing?

Novice monk: Answering the phone.

Venerable Master (before the assembly): What could be more important than requesting that the Dharma be spoken? You have to be most sincere and earnest when requesting Dharma and that the Buddhas throughout the ten directions will come before us. How can you cultivate if you don't have the slightest respect toward the Dharma? Kneel down!

(The Venerable Master proceeded with his two-and-a-half hour class on the Records of Water Mirror Reflecting Heaven without telling the novice monk to stand up.)

ଚଠ୯ଓ

Q: May I ask about how my future will turn out?

A: Ask yourself whether you're compassionate. There's no need to inquire about your future

ଚଠ୯ଓ

Q: Obviously I only say what I think is right.

A: Then your frankness got you where you are now!

ಋಞ

Q: Two Bhikshus would like to fast for eighteen days...

A: It would be better if they just worked hard on sweeping the floor. There's no need to fast.

ಋಞ

Q: Will I die from hunger or cold when I become old?

A: What a pathetic way of thinking!

ಋಞ

Q: Why is it appropriate for Guanshiyin Bodhisattva to look, look, and look all day long, but I can't?

A: The way you look and the way Guanshiyin Bodhisattva looks are different. Guanshiyin Bodhisattva looks inwardly while you look out.

ಋಞ

Venerable Master: It's wrong to have opened my mouth and it's wrong if I keep my mouth shut. You tell me what I should do.

The disciple couldn't come up with a response.

ಐಂಞ

Q: Isn't it a waste that the Master has lots of property but they're all vacant?

A: There are plenty of things that are wasted in this world.

ಐಂಞ

Q: The Master says, "I'm not afraid of people coming and I'm not afraid of people running away either. It's the same whether they came or not; it's just the same whether they run away or not." Why?

A: *The Master answers his own rhetorical question,* "The Dharma Realm is mine. People can run far away and yet they cannot run outside the Dharma Realm. If they were able to run outside the Dharma Realm, they would have [succeeded] in their getaway. They haven't escaped if they haven't reached the outside of the Dharma Realm. Like "the monkey king" whose one flip goes as far as 18,000 miles, but can never get out of the Buddha's palm."

೮೦೮ಚ

Venerable Master: Don't pick only the good stuff to eat. Don't be greedy for form, scent, and taste. Since you have enough food, eat only about eighty percent full. How can you cultivate if you can't even let go of food?

The disciple was speechless.

೮೦೮ಚ

Venerable Master: Whose turn is it to give a talk tonight?

(People pushed a disciple out from the crowd.)

Disciple: I don't know Chinese and didn't bring pen and paper.

Venerable Master: Just say what's in your heart when you're giving a Dharma talk. Don't be scared that people will think you're a poor speaker. Just tell the truth and there will naturally be people who appreciate it.

෨෦ఴ

Q: What kind of talk is wise?

A: To be truly wise, we would speak simply, clearly, and to the point. Don't say any more than is necessary.

෨෦ఴ

Q: I'm asking about how to cultivate.

A: Why cultivate?

෨෦ఴ

Q: How can we disciples work on behalf of Buddhism?

A: The four types of monastic and lay disciples

must complement and support each other, working together cooperatively for the sake of Buddhism.

ജഅ

A disciple is thinking: There are so many excellent offerings, why don't we eat more of them and really enjoy them?

Venerable Master: Okay, eat more, cultivate more, stir up more trouble—you always want more; you never get enough of anything.

ജഅ

Q: Have I misinterpreted the Vajra Sutra?

A: Mull over its meaning.

ജഅ

Venerable Master: What are the Four Qualities of Mindfulness?

A disciple: Oh, I don't know.

V enerable Master: What are the Five Roots?

A disciple: Oh, are they the five sticks *(which has the same pronunciation as "roots" in Chinese)* of incense I burned yesterday?

V enerable Master: What are the Six Paramitas?

A disciple: Oh, I'm just one person; I don't have six stomachs *(which has the same pronunciation as "Paramitas" in Chinese)*.

V enerable Master: What are the Eight Noble Paths?

A disciple: Probably eight large roads!

V enerable Master: What are the Ten Powers?

A disciple: Are they ten different kinds of powers?

V enerable Master: What are the Eighteen Shared Dharmas?

A disciple: I don't have a clue.

Venerable Master: How can you improve if you don't know the answers to any question though you have studied the Buddhadharma?

৵জ

Q: Master, someone wants to become a monk. First, because he wants to repay the Buddha's kindness, second, to repay the Master's kindness...

A: I have lots of disciples, but very few really repay my kindness.

৵জ

A disciple's praise of a picture of Bodhidharma:

> *Do you know who he is?*
> *Bodhidharma the elder patriarch,*
> *the man of the Way*
> *From the Western Land whence eastward he came.*
> *Sitting before a wall for nine years,*

He saw his nature and understood the mind.
Oh but actually, he was being a busybody!

*V*enerable Master: You still haven't gotten it. To see his nature and understand the mind implies that there are two dharmas; but the Buddhadharma points to nonduality. Understanding the mind is just seeing one's nature.

&OCB

Q: Will the Master please instruct me on how to be a person?

A: You've still got a person.

&OCB

*V*enerable Master: In my empty hand, I'm clutching a hatchet.

> *I walk while riding on a buffalo*
> *For someone crossing a bridge*
> *The bridge appears to move,*
> *while the water runs still.*
> *Can you do that?*

A Disciple: No.

V enerable Master: What a waste for you to have followed Buddhism for several decades! *(He reaches for the disciple's shirtsleeve as he finishes talking.)* I hang on to a sleeve that leaves me empty-handed.

ৰাৰ্ঙ্গ

A Disciple: What's the use of talking about it?

V enerable Master: What's the use of not talking about it?

ৰাৰ্ঙ্গ

T he Venerable Master turns his head that so he is looking at a monk's notes upside down.

Q : What is this?

A Disciple: My notes.

ৰাৰ্ঙ্গ

W hile the Venerable Master is giving a talk, a disciple is entertaining a false thought off the stage: It's so hard to earn a Ph.D., should I attempt it?

*V*enerable Master *(in the talk)*: Some people are really stupid; they don't enjoy studying and yet they want to go and get a Ph.D...

This disciple thought he was just that way. He didn't enjoy studying and yet he still wanted to earn a doctorate degree. He would only cause himself distress. So stupid! He immediately decided to not pursue the degree.

⊗∽⊗

*I*n 1991, a proposal to expand the City of Ten Thousand Buddhas was denied by the local government. The disciples responsible for the application dejectedly asked the Venerable Master:

Q: Why didn't it pass?

A: Because you don't have enough virtue. That's why it failed.

ೞ౪

Venerable Master: Is there a problem with the search for monasteries?

A Disciple: Yes. I could never find [a suitable] one. I don't know how to find one. I've been searching for four years, from 1992 to 1995.

Venerable Master: To build a monastery, you must have a vision that is far and wide, a plan that will cover the next century. You have to find a place that is big enough to accommodate future expansions and is conveniently located in city centers. You have to find a facility that can be used comprehensively and allows for more stories to be added. If a monastery is in a high-riser, it ought to be the one on the top floor. Businesses on the lower floors below the monastery must be larger than 10,000 square foot.

ೞ౪

*O*nce one of the Master's disciples removed an important guest. The Master scolded his disciple so harshly that the student nearly wanted to pack up his stuff and leave.

A Disciple: I feel so ashamed. What I did was wrong, unhelpful, and really pathetic. I should die.

*V*enerable Master: You won't die. Quit lying to yourself. For you to go away and die would be letting you off easy! You should change your bad habits. Where's that Sutra on the Comprehensive Extinction of Dharmas? Bring it over and read it to me! Since you've already left the householder's life with me, you can't act the way you used to. You must cultivate now. You're the Buddha's disciple, a member of the Buddha's family. Don't you realize how your every move is important? In this country, you represent the Buddha, Dharma, and Sangha, do you understand? You're no longer living for yourself. How could you be so careless and so selfish? Don't you see the path that you've chosen? How could you act like someone who is just hanging around and waiting for the next meal? As the Buddha's disciple, you have to be a role model for humans and gods. You have to be outstanding! You have to undertake what others cannot undertake, eat what others cannot eat, suffer what others cannot suffer, do what others cannot do, and bear what others cannot bear. This is the only way for you to pass the test. You must consider the propagation of Dharma your personal duty; otherwise, the Buddhadharma will never become rooted in this country.

Buddhism

Q: What can we do to help Buddhism prosper?

A: Cultivate by holding the Five Precepts, and practicing humaneness, a sense of fairness, propriety, wisdom, and trustworthiness. This way, little by little, Buddhism will prosper.

೮೦೮೩

Q: Out of the 84,000 Dharma doors in Buddhism, which one is the best and most wonderful?

A: All of the 84,000 Dharma doors are the best. Not one of them is second place. Why do I say that? The 84,000 Dharma doors treat the 84,000 kinds of shortcomings of living beings. Every living being has his or her own particular faults. Therefore, the best practice is the one that cures one's faults.

೮೦೮೩

Q: Resolutions are easy to make at the beginning, but how do we see them through?

A: We should hang the words "birth and death" from our eyebrows in order to maintain our perseverance. If we retreat, it must be because we forgot our initial resolve.

ൈൖ

Q: Buddhism talks about how things are "unspeakably unspeakable." Exactly why are things unspeakable?

A: Why are you speaking now?

ൈൖ

Q: What is the difference between false thoughts and vows? How would we know if our vows are false thoughts?

A: If our vows benefit others, then they serve a purpose even though they are false thoughts. Beyond that, you should get rid of false thoughts.

ൈൖ

Q: Confucius had three thousand disciples, seventy-two of whom were proficient in the six arts. What abilities should one possess in our society today to be considered a paragon of virtue?

A: "To have virtue is to be truly rich. Those who have no virtue are the most impoverished." A paragon of virtue does not kill, does not steal, does not indulge in sexual misconduct, does not lie, and does not take intoxicants.

୫୦୯୧

Q: Master, what are the special features of the Weiyang School? How can we expand it?

A: The Weiyang School is very ordinary; there's nothing special about it. The Weiyang School doesn't have any plans to expand. We should just have strong moral characters.

୫୦୯୧

Q: Which Sutra is suitable for beginners?

A: Any Sutra is suitable.

Q: What can I do to help Buddhist monasteries?

A: You help monasteries by not destroying them. You help monasteries by supporting them.

Q: How are the Schools of Weiyang, Lingji, Caodong, and others different?

A: There is no real difference. These groups are composed of practitioners who are average people who have not become Bodhisattvas yet.

Q: We hear that the merit from liberating beings is the greatest. Is that correct?

A: All the merit done for Buddhism is equal.

We must liberate life out of compassion. If we were interested in merit, then we would not have much merit to speak of. It is incorrect to say that such and such a merit is the greatest, because such distinctions are bound to entice people to earn merit for the wrong reasons.

ଔଓ

Q: A certain Dharma Master said that Buddhists do not need to attend morning and evening services. Is that correct?

A: What he advocates is his problem. Since morning and evening services are unnecessary to him, then everything else must be unnecessary too. It must be okay for him to not eat, not drink, and not sleep. Has he reached the level of non-cultivation and non-certification? He can only say such things if he were to have reached that level; otherwise, he shouldn't say such things.

ଔଓ

Q: Is it necessary to choose a day for putting a Bodhisattva statue in place and a direction that the statue should face?

A: It is not necessary to choose a day and a direction. It is fine as long as the Bodhisattva statue is elevated to a position above waste-level. Demons and ghosts think about checking on dates and positions for this kind of thing.

ଽଔଓଔ

Q: How can we rescue our deceased ancestors and others?

A: Only preeminent monks who have cultivated virtue and samadhi can alter the suffering of the deceased and thereby help them to enter the heavens. When Meditation Master Lungku of the Ming Dynasty saved the mother of Emperor Wanli, for instance, he said from the podium, "I was not going to come here, but you insisted I do. Without giving rise to a thought, may you transcend the three realms."

With these lines, the emperor's mother entered the heavens.

৪০০৪

Q: Are we acting in accord with the Dharma when we burn fake money with the Rebirth Mantra written on them?

A: Why burn that stuff in the first place? You think about it. Is that money real or fake? What use is there in burning papers with the Rebirth Mantra on them, anyway? Once burned, the paper turns into ash. How could you think that it can be used as money?

৪০০৪

Q: Will we be affected physically and mentally if we reveal our date of birth to those on a deviant path?

A: As long as your mind is straight, then for you, nothing will be deviant. If your mind is deviant, every path would be an evil path.

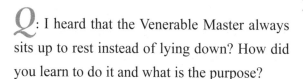

ಬಂಆ

Q: I heard that the Venerable Master always sits up to rest instead of lying down? How did you learn to do it and what is the purpose?

A: Nobody told you that I always lie down to rest instead of sitting up? There is no set rule for this. If you want to sit, then you sit; if you want to lie down, then you lie down. It does not matter whether or not others say you are sitting up or lying down. Why should we be attached to something like this? Anything that we're attached to becomes a burden to us. The important thing for us cultivators is not to be troubled at any time, whether sitting up or lying down. It is important to get rid of afflictions.

ಬಂಆ

Q: All conditioned dharmas are like dreams and illusions, bubbles and shadows. So, what are Unconditioned Dharmas?

A: For a detailed description of the six Unconditioned Dharmas, you may check the Shastra on the Door to Understanding the Hundred Dharmas. The one hundred dharmas consist of: The Eleven Form Dharmas, The Eight Mind Dharmas, The 51 Dharmas Interactive with the Mind, The 24 Non-Interactive Activity Dharmas, and The Six Unconditioned Dharmas.

৪০৫৪

Q: Please talk about awakening to the views of all Buddhas.

A: To awaken to the views of Buddhas is to know how Buddhas became Buddhas and to have wisdom of the Buddhas. This is nothing too esoteric. We awaken to the views of Buddhas by being like the Buddhas and practicing the four qualities of the limitless mind: kindness, compassion, generosity, and equanimity.

৪০৫৪

Q: Is the Buddhadharma that you talk about inclusive, embodying all the various sects/schools of Buddhism?

A: That's the way it is if that's the way you think. If you want to exclude them, they're excluded; if you want to include them, they're included. This is not fixed. "The Buddha proclaimed Dharma with one sound, but different living beings understood differently." "Wise ones tend to see wisdom occurring; humane ones tend to see humaneness occurring. Profound individuals tend to see profundity while shallow individuals tend to see shallowness."

෨෮෯

Q: Which is the best practice out of the 84,000 Dharma doors? Which is the most supreme?

A: The most supreme Dharma door is one that you find most suitable; the weakest Dharma door is the one you find most useless.

☙☼ℭ

Q: How can I possess the ability to select the right Dharma?

A: I don't have the ability to select the right Dharma either, so how can I tell you?

☙☼ℭ

Q: How can we cultivate to escape birth and death?

A: Eat, dress, and sleep.

☙☼ℭ

Q: Is it effective to have sutras and mantras printed on fake money for the deceased and also to burn them?

A: The paper money turns into ash when you burn it. How would I know whether ash is effective or not [as money in the underworld]? Let's suppose it is effective; so does that mean all Westerner hungry ghosts are poor because they don't believe in burning paper money?

ઠઉ**જ**

Q: Master, what is your view on the styles of monasteries?

A: I don't like gaudy monasteries painted red and green, like women wearing bright red lipstick. The basic rule for the construction of monasteries is that they be labor-effective and durable.

ઠઉ**જ**

Q: Why do people worship the Monkey King instead of the Great Master Hsuan Zhuang of the Tang Dynasty? Did the Monkey King really exist?

A: People like the Monkey King because of his golden baton, his acrobatic ability to do somersaults and travel to the heavens and hells. The characters of the Monkey King, the pig, and the novice monk really did exist, but as invisible spirits who protected the monk of the

Tang Dynasty as he traveled to India for Sutras. They were not visible to ordinary people. They were spirits without physical form.

ഇൻൻ

Q: By praying, we develop inner spiritual energy that could benefit all things. So do we still need to do good deeds on the outside?

A: Cultivation should be a balance between developing inner merit and outward results. When we're doing external merit, we are not attached to the attainment of such merit. We can help ourselves by cultivating virtue within, purifying our thoughts, and lessening our desires. If we can stop being greedy, we will be helping others.

ഇൻൻ

Q: Master, I would like to know what the Buddhadharma really is.

A: The fact that you are asking this question is because of your Buddha nature. You would not be asking this question if it were not for that. You deserve to be beaten a hundred times for not knowing that this is the Buddha nature.

හිල

Q: If the Buddhas were compassionate and omnipotent, why is there still suffering (earthquake, fire, war, famine, sickness, etc.) in the world?

A: According to your line of thinking, you would say that the Buddhas are not omnipotent or compassionate. I don't dare say that.

හිල

Q: Who are the original ancestors of all sentient beings, including animals that fly and swim, flowers, grass and trees?

A: The Buddha nature is our ancestor.

හිල

Q: Is the so-called possession by spirits real? Is it evil?

A: Didn't I mention earlier that there are all kinds of ghosts, spirits, demons, and ogres? Whether you recognize them or not depends on whether you have wisdom.

§✿§

Q: Where did human beings come from?

A: Have you seen those bugs in rice containers? Those bugs appear all of a sudden and we don't know where they came from. In the same way, people are born from true emptiness.

§✿§

Q: Master, how do I deeply feel the pain caused by the wheel of life and death? How do I bring forth the resolve to cultivate?

A: How can I make you feel pain when you don't?

§✿§

Q: Human beings are so tiny in comparison to the universe, and yet we lord over the universe. What is the tiniest thing there is?

A: Human beings are not tiny and the universe is not huge.

❀❀❀

Q: Can we offer music with Sanskrit lyrics to the Buddhas?

A: Anything is fine. Anything that you like can be offered to the Buddhas.

❀❀❀

Q: How can we avoid meeting obstacles as we study Buddhism?

A: We will encounter obstacles when studying Buddhism. The difference lies with your samadhi power. If you were to have samadhi power and wisdom, you would be able to easily resolve any potential problem that comes your way. It would not become a problem for you. If you are extremely stupid, a mosquito bite is a problem, and the buzzing of a fly is problematic too.

৪৩

Q: What was the Buddha's attitude toward life?

A: One of compassion, joy, generosity, and equanimity.

৪৩

Q: Does destiny really exist? Do people have the ability to control their own fate?

A: Superior individuals realize they can mold
their own destiny.
Determining my own destiny,
I acquire my own blessings.
Disasters and blessings occur only
because people brought them about.
Retributions and rewards follow us around
like shadows.

Superior people create and change their destinies, whereas most average people think that everything is predestined. If you have faith and perseverance, you can leap from the level of an average person to the level of a Buddha. If everything were predestined, we could very well get our fortune read before we even start to study Buddhism just to see if we have a chance at becoming Buddhas. None of the fortunes and misfortunes in our lives are set in stone. If you are an extremely good person or an extremely bad person, your destiny will be different from the average person because what you have done has gone beyond the bounds of an average person.

ಇಂಛ

Q: What's the difference between saving human beings, ghosts, and demons?

A: Why would you ask if they were the same?

Q: Why are there demons?

A: The demons in our self-nature attract the ones outside. The demons of our self-nature are greed, anger and delusion. They are the poisons of our self-nature and attract external demons.

ðŏC3

Q: 1. How do we make ourselves bold and vigorous? 2. How do I overcome the habit of eating and sleeping too much? (A beautician asked these questions.)

A: 1. By truly becoming a beautiful person. 2. By not eating, which will lead to not sleeping. The less you eat, the less you sleep.

ðŏC3

Q: When we hear a nice song, can we offer it to the Buddhas or Bodhisattvas? How do we offer it?

A: You can sing it, but you need to be sure that it is not suggestive. It has to be proper. At the City of Ten Thousand Buddhas, we also present Buddhist songs to the Buddhas. For example, the praises that we sing before the Buddhas are songs of offering. The Dharma Flower Sutra makes it very clear that melodic songs and incantations can be offerings for Buddhas.

৵৹টঠ

Q: Many people don't see any results from their cultivation despite having done so for a long time. Is the Buddhadharma not working? Maybe the Sutras and mantras don't have the power to make miracles happen?

A: That's not it. It is because you are not sincere. You cultivate in a sloppy manner and only go through the motions. You simply do what everyone else does. You haven't been sincere.

৵৹টঠ

Q: I read this line in a magazine, "If we can't become Buddhas from studying Buddhism in this lifetime, then we have not been studying correctly." What is the Master's opinion with regard to this statement?

A: If you have been studying incorrectly, then learn what is correct! "We should not have any books if we believe in them entirely." I don't know about magazines and I can't write articles. I'm no expert when it comes to magazines because I have no time to read them.

༄༅༅

Q: When my parents passed away in mainland China, I wasn't able to visit their gravesite. Am I right in thinking that they wouldn't receive the effect of my bowing to the Buddhas here in Taiwan?

A: If you are sincere, they will receive the effect no matter how far away. If you are insincere, they will not receive anything even if they were right before your eyes.

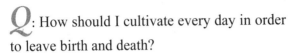

Q: How should I cultivate every day in order to leave birth and death?

A: Cultivation is about "watching our every move; staying close to home (the mind) whether walking, standing, sitting, or lying down."

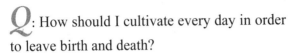

Q: What should I do if I want to recite Sutras but don't have a Buddha statue in the house?

A: You must first learn how to read if you want to recite Sutras. Once you can read, you can naturally recite Sutras.

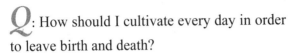

Q: Why is it that some people use money as a measure for judging which Buddhist has cultivated well or poorly? How do we find the real path to Buddhahood?

A: The real path to Buddhahood is the poorest. Such Buddhists are not interested in money; they don't want it.

⊰⊱

Q: Please tell me how a beginner should study Buddhism? How do we choose wise advisors and the right place for cultivation? How do we judge whether a dharma is proper?

A: There is no one right way. You have to have the ability to choose the proper Dharma for yourself. If the Dharma is genuine, you should not treat it as if it were false; and if false, you shouldn't treat it as if it were genuine. That would be enough.

⊰⊱

Q: Why isn't there a Dharma Realm for demons?

A: The demons are like bandits. They wander everywhere like a team of guerillas, having no permanent place to live or anyone to manage them. Demons are a group similar to bandits. Bandits are human beings, but since not everyone is a bandit, there is no realm for bandits.

ಶಿಂಬ

Q: Can people be possessed by spirits?

A: Please ask someone who is possessed by a spirit this question. I am not possessed by spirits. Even if I knew the answer, I would not talk about it.

ಶಿಂಬ

Q: What is more important, to save myself or others? Which is of higher priority?

A: Neither one is more nor less important. They're of equal importance. It is a mistake on your part to want to differentiate between them by order of importance.

ಶಿಂಬ

Q: Can Buddhists trade stocks?

A: Some Buddhists murder, steal, engage in sexual misconduct, lie, and drink alcohol. Do you think they should be doing these things?

৪০গ্ত

Q: What is the reason behind burning paper money for our ancestors?

A: If this were reasonable, all the Westerners would be poor. You should look into the truth and never be superstitious.

৪০গ্ত

Q: How do we teach and transform living beings who are difficult to tame and subdue? Is there really an end to this world?

A: We should be extremely patient in teaching and transforming them. The day each person dies is the end of the world for that person.

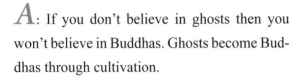

ဆာ

Q: Do you believe in ghosts?

A: If you don't believe in ghosts then you won't believe in Buddhas. Ghosts become Buddhas through cultivation.

Q: What are the basics in cultivation?

A: We should not have so many discursive thoughts. Don't think so much. "A hundred things occur because of the movement of a thought; ten thousand things cease with the stopping of a thought." Everything can happen because of one thought. If not one thought appears, then the entire substance manifests and nothing will happen. The basic issue here has to do with thoughts of desire.

ဆာ

Q: How should people new to Buddhism cultivate and maintain themselves?

A: Eat, dress, and sleep.

&oc&

Q: So, how do we cultivate?

A: You should cultivate according to your ability, doing what you can and not forcing yourself into doing what you can't.

&oc&

Q: Are mediums, channelers, etc. part of the Buddhadharma?

A: All dharmas are the Buddhadharma; none can be obtained. Or we could say that all dharmas are no Buddhadharma. Anyway, we must let go of any attachment as we study Buddhism: sweep away all dharmas and leave every mark.

&oc&

Q: by The Venerable Master: What is ultimately real? Everyone try speaking up!

Buddhist: Cultivation is real!

The Venerable Master: Then why don't you cultivate? If you're looking for what is real in the world, you will not find it. Cultivation may be real, but it's invisible. What you see are just the appearances. Truth is soundless and scent-free, formless and colorless. Nevertheless, we must find the true in the false. Don't search for the real by leaving the false.

ಸಿದ್ಧ

Q: Some people say that the idea of a "soul" doesn't exist in Buddhism. Is that correct?

A: Some people may say that, but this statement can't represent the Buddha's teachings in their entirety. I have never heard of such a theory and I am a Buddhist.

ಸಿದ್ಧ

Q: What is the biggest problem with Buddhism?

A: The biggest problem is greed, exploitation, and selfishness.

৪৩৫৩

Q: How do we make the Proper Dharma live long in the world?

A: To have the Proper Dharma live long in the world, you must not fight, not be greedy, not be selfish, not pursue personal advantages, and not lie.

৪৩৫৩

Q: My son asked me how many preeminent monks have converted tigers and lions and given them refuge. Also, what would polar bears eat if they were to take refuge? The North Pole is too cold for any vegetables.

A: Eat ice! Eat snow! What if they were at the South Pole? Eat ice! Eat snow!

ಬಂಣ

Q: Some people say that we can believe in Buddhism without having to take refuge with the Triple Jewel. Is that right?

A: Take education, for instance. If you want to graduate from elementary school, you must finish your courses for elementary school. If you want a high school diploma, you have to finish your high school courses. If you want to obtain degrees for bachelors, masters, or doctorates, you would naturally have to complete the required curriculum for those levels, pass your tests, and receive your degree. The same principle applies to taking refuge with the Triple Jewel.

ಬಂಣ

Q: Some lay people tell us that the reason they don't advance but retreat is because their karmic obstruction has shown up. How should we respond to them if this kind of karma is fixed? Do we force them to continue to be diligent?

A: That depends on the situation at the time. Prescribe medicine according to the specific illness. Afflictions and Bodhi are like ice and water. Afflictions are Bodhi. One is born after one is put to death. It is right to bear what one really cannot bear and to go through what one really cannot go through. No need to corner yourself; there's no dead end.

၄၁၄၃

Q: Can we cross over our late ancestors by reciting Sutras?

A: Somewhat. One-seventh of the merit will accrue to the deceased; six-sevenths, to the living who create the merit.

၄၁၄၃

Q: Is it in accord with the Dharma to make Buddhist songs like popular music? Will it invite criticism?

A: If you're afraid of being criticized by others, then you might as well not do anything. Just ask yourself if anything good happens in the world without criticism. If you're scared of criticism, then don't do it. If you're not afraid of criticism, then go on and forge ahead.

෴

Q: I would like to ask the Master what kind of practice I should do to help me have more faith.

A: Faith can be likened to reacting to the five flavors. The various practices that the Buddha described can be likened to these flavors: sour, sweet, bitter, spicy, and salty. No flavor can be called the best. Everyone has a favorite flavor, that's all.

෴

Q: This path is so arduous. Will I be able to persist to the end and not retreat?

A: You will reach your destination as long as you are bold and vigorous, strong and indefatigable.

ဆာလ

Q: Your Buddhadharma seems different than that of Asia's.

A: During the Dharma-ending Age, Buddhism focuses on superficialities. Corruption and deficiencies are rampant in Buddhism. If we don't rescue it immediately by revolutionizing it, then the lifeline of the Buddhadharma will also be cut off. We need to improve many different aspects of Buddhism for this time and age.

ဆာလ

Q: What are some guiding principles for propagating Buddhism in the United States?

A: The most fundamental are the Six Great Guiding Principles: no greed, no fighting, no seeking, no selfishness, no pursuit of self-benefit, and no lies. These six mirrors reveal monsters by reflecting them. These six pestles also tame demons. If we can base ourselves on these Six Great Guiding Principles at all times, then demons, heretics, and phonies will have nowhere to hide. They will be exposed for who they really are. Our principle will create more proper energy for the universe and shatter and eliminate the heightened violence and toxic resentment that permeate the entire globe.

଼ୠ୲ୠଷ

Q: How do we tell the difference between good teachers and bad teachers?

A: That's easy. Just observe to see if he is greedy for money. Is he licentious? Let these two be your standards of measurement.

଼ୠ୲ୠଷ

Q: Will the Master predict when Buddhism will flourish in the United States?

A: It's already flourishing. Don't be discontent! Isn't Buddhism flourishing since the number of Buddhists is relatively large in a country that is predominantly Christians and Catholics?

૪૦૦૪

Q: How can we make the Buddhadharma flourish in the countries of the West?

A: Cultivate according to the Dharma! Keep the Five Precepts and practice the eight virtues. Do it bit by bit, and it will flourish!

૪૦૦૪

Q: Why can't Buddhism be simpler so that more people can understand it at once?

A: Why don't we think of ways for kids to go to work as soon as they're born?

૪૦૦૪

Q: A national leader once said, "Buddhism is the humaneness that saves the world. Buddhism is the mother of philosophy. Studying Buddhism can fix the slant of science." Why did he say this?

A: Buddhism is true science. Before science was developed, several thousand years ago, the Buddha said, "The Buddha sees 84,000 insects in a bowl of water. If one doesn't recite this mantra, it is as if one is eating living beings' meat." From this, we can tell that although the Buddha didn't have a microscope or magnifier, he knew there were numerous microorganisms in a bowl of water. It wasn't until recently that people have proven this to be correct. So the level of people's wisdom today is far below the level of the Buddha's wisdom. That national leader may have said that Buddhism can fix the slant of science, but my opinion is that Buddhism not only can fix the slant of science, Buddhism contains science while science cannot contain Buddhism."

Q: What is the Vinaya?

A: The Six Great Guiding Principles of the City of Ten Thousand Buddhas are the Vinaya. To avoid fighting is to avoid violating the precept against killing; to avoid being greedy is to avoid violating the precept against stealing; and to avoid being selfish is to avoid violating the precept against lying. Why do we lie? We go around telling lies because we want our own interests served. To avoid pursuing self-benefit is to avoid violating the precept against taking intoxicants. Drinkers think that drinking is good for their health because alcohol makes their blood circulate faster. When they're drunk, they feel so high that they think they've become gods. Drinkers' false thoughts and self-interests are troublemakers. To avoid lying is a principle already included in the above five items, but to caution everyone especially, we emphasize the liability of lying by adding the sixth principle as a precaution.

೩೦೦೪

Q: What happens if we are illiterate and do not understand the words to the text?

A: This is easy, just learn! You can ask others if you don't understand! To draw near good teachers is to find good friends!

೩೦೦೪

Q: Why should I adhere to the Five Precepts if I haven't received them?

A: The Five Precepts are the precepts of our inherent nature. You should keep them whether you have received them or not. Receiving the precepts is a phenomenon while keeping the precepts is a noumenon. You must keep the precepts purely so that the noumenon becomes perfected.

೩೦೦೪

Q: How can we realize Buddhahood soon?

A: First learn to be human and deal with different situations.

೫೦೧೪

Q: Some people think that Buddhism is a passive religion. Will you please expound on their perspective?

A: It would be wrong to think that Buddhism is passive. Buddhism is most pro-active. It's just that most of us don't understand this kind of pro-activity. In today's world that is fragile, chaotic, and war-torn, people are in a daze all day, oblivious to the fact that their lives could end the next day. Buddhists, however, remain completely calm in this state of affairs, still cultivating and doing the work that they should be doing. Take the Sangha at the City of Ten Thousand Buddhas, for instance, which grounds itself in Buddhist traditions, getting up at 3:30 a.m. to participate in the 4 a.m. service. There may be universal bowing, meditation, Sutra recitation, a repentance ceremony or individual work after the morning service. Think about it, is it passive to get up so early and work hard on cultivation all day long?

෨෬

Q: We can only cultivate the Buddhadharma by having no desires, but this world would make no progress unless there were desires. How do ordinary people balance the two?

A: When you say there's progress only because of desires, what kind of progress might that be? So what if there is progress? How is that beneficial?

෨෬

Q: What kind of status and role do women have in Buddhism? If they were to learn the Buddhadharma from you, how should they apply themselves?

A: There's no difference between men and women in Buddhism. There are only rules in Buddhism. Women have more rules to follow than men do because women have the habit of being picky over the smallest things. Men are unrefined and more imprecise. So Buddhism is about equality, but each gender has its set of rules that they have to follow.

ชอดช

Q: How can we tell who is truly a teacher who understands?

A: To tell, just check to see if he contends and if he is greedy. Check to see if he pursues only personal advantages. See if he always lies but claims that he is being expedient. If you still consider people like that to be good advisors, then you can't tell right from wrong.

ชอดช

Q: The Vajra Sutra says, "Thoughts of the

past cannot be gotten at, thoughts of the present cannot be gotten at, and thoughts of the future cannot be gotten at." Could the text be explained by using the line, "give rise to the mind that is nowhere produced"?

A: Thoughts of the past have already gone, where will one find those thoughts? Thoughts of the present do not stop either, so where are those present thoughts? Thoughts of the future have not yet come! Therefore, thoughts of the past, present, and future cannot be gotten at means that we should not entertain any false thinking.

৪০০৪

By a student: Will the Venerable Master please tell me how I can strengthen my determination?

Venerable Master: How do you obtain determination? Why do you want determination?

Student: I'm not strong enough.

Venerable Master: Who took it away?

Student: It's right here in me.

Venerable Master: If it's right there inside you, why are you asking me?

Student: Well, should I just practice on my own?

Venerable Master: Since you have it, just turn around, find it, and use it! You're asking me, but how can I teach you to be strong? Your determination belongs to you while my determination belongs to me. By asking me this question, are you going outside yourself for answers? Aren't you asking a blind man for directions?

Student: Maybe I have not lost it, but I just want to strengthen it.

Venerable Master: When did you lose it? And why are you so determined when you're chasing after women?

Student: I understand.

(The crowd laughs.)

Venerable Master: If you've got determination in that area, why don't you have determination in this area?

Student: Now I've got it.

ಹೋಗ

Q: What does "the mutual unknowing of dharmas" mean?

A: Do you need to ask? They don't know one another! Do you think dharmas can be cognizant of one another? Do dharmas have awareness?

ಹೋಗ

By a student: You say each religion has its strengths and weaknesses. What are the weaknesses of Buddhism?

A: There are many weaknesses. Cheating people! Claiming others' money for themselves! These are all weaknesses. Buddhists should not exploit relationships and try to get people to make offerings to them. These types of Buddhists let their blessings slip away. Buddhist monastics should not touch money, but why do some monastics have so much money in their pockets? They're suppose to be eating one meal at midday, staying under a tree at any given location for a limited time only, remaining uninterested in valuables, owning no possessions, and just going on their alms rounds barefoot and eating whatever they receive. That ought to be enough. So why do they live in high risers? Why do they live in such luxurious housing facilities? Eat such delicious food? Dress so nicely? What does this mean? Are these weaknesses?

࿐

Q: Why doesn't Buddhism build more monasteries and give more Sutra lectures? Would more people learn about Buddhism that way?

A: Buddhism has odious aspects, too, sometimes. How is it odious? In China, Buddhists want to rule their individual turfs. They're in chaos, like sand that has been strewn about.

Q: Some people say that it seems like there are more Buddhas than human beings.

A: Buddhas do not have conflicts. They are all one. However many Buddhas there are, there are just as many human beings. Human beings, however, fight with each other.

Q: How do people who believe in and accept the Buddhadharma protect their Bodhi resolve?

A: Who told you not to protect it?

Q: Buddhism says "All beings have the Buddha nature." Why are beings so lost that they need to continue to suffer now?

A: All beings have the Buddha nature; all beings also have the ghost nature; beings also have the animal nature; beings also have the nature of gods and of Bodhisattvas. Beings come complete with such potential. But most only know to go downhill and not to move up. It is said, "The superior person understands what is lofty while the petty person understands what is base." Beings are greedy for visible and tangible objects in the world. They think that eating, drinking, and making merry are real. They don't recognize the happiness that is in their true and inherent nature. Therefore, there are actually "two paths are one of good and one of evil. Some cultivate goodness. Others commit evil." You say that living beings are all lost, but there are those who are not lost. There are those who seriously cultivate, taking one step at a time and working as hard as they possibly can. So you can't say that all beings are lost.

ॐॐ

Q: The Buddhadharma is new to me. I would like to know to which school you belong.

A: Gold Mountain Monastery belongs to Buddhism. It doesn't belong to a particular school or sect of Buddhism. It is Buddhism that has no schools or sects.

ഇൽൽ

Q: "The monkey king" was born from a rock. Why did a rock give birth to that monkey?

A: "The monkey king" is a demon; plenty of similar cases exist. The monkey king was probably experiencing some problems with his thinking skandha during his cultivation, so he became a monkey that could bore his way through to the heavens and dig his way into the earth. He symbolizes demons described in the Shurangama Sutra.

ഇൽൽ

Q: The Venerable Master says that the Buddha's teachings are about wisdom. What is a Buddha? What is great wisdom? Great kindness and compassion? Great humaneness?

A: These questions cannot be answered in a few words. The word Buddha is half of a transliterated Sanskrit word. "Buddhaya" is the entire word. It's "Buddha" in English, which sounds like "Not Big" in Chinese, so I've called it that too. Buddhas are not big, but are they small? They are not small either. Buddhas are like people, they are not any bigger, they just have superior wisdom. Buddhas successfully cultivate the Three Bodies, the Four Wisdoms, the Five Eyes, and the Six Penetrations successfully. Buddhas are absolutely capable. Buddhas have terrific wisdom, which is why they are immensely compassionate. They always have the greatest energy and resources; they are never lacking. No one can compare to Buddhas in terms of abilities. Most people are limited in their capabilities; but Buddhas' capabilities are unlimited, which is also why they have boundless kindness and compassion, boundless joy, and boundless equanimity. Kindness, compassion, joy, and equanimity are the four qualities of the Buddhas' Boundless Mind. Most people have limited kindness, compassion, joy, and equanimity. They are not like Buddhas. Buddhas can give up what other people cannot give up. They are "greatly kind to those with whom they have no affinities; and greatly compassionate because they consider everyone the same." What is kindness? What is compassion? Kindness makes others happy. Compassion ends others' suffering.

༺༻

Q: Why can the wealth of Dharma be damaged? Why will merit and virtue end?

A: That's because you use your consciousness, in particular, to calculate, guess, and discriminate. You only expend effort on your consciousness, therefore you will harm your wealth of Dharma and end your merit and virtue.

༺༻

Q: Does a Buddhist disciple who has received the Five Precepts and the Bodhisattva Precepts have to uphold them with care and be a lifelong vegetarian?

A: Of course! What's the use of receiving the precepts if you are not going to keep them?

৪৩০৪

Disciple: We should organize non-religious activities more often so that more people will come to believe in the Buddha.

A: Anyone who is my disciple should cultivate well. I am more concerned about quality than quantity in order to avoid violating the law of cause and effect.

৪৩০৪

Q: What kind of Buddha is a Japanese Buddha?

A: A Japanese Buddha!

Reporter: Is the Buddhism in Nepal, India, China, Japan, and other countries different? Will Buddhism in America be different from Buddhism in Asia?

A: Yes, Buddhism in America will be different. To propagate the Buddhaharma in America, we, of course, have to consider the habits and uniqueness of Americans. For instance, Americans will recite Sutras in English because they don't necessarily know Chinese. So we have to translate Buddhist scriptures into English. Also, Buddhism requires monastics to be vegetarians and celibate. Some Americans left the householder's life on impulse, and yet couldn't tolerate the lonely monastic life. They may return to laylife, but they shouldn't ruin the rules laid down by Buddhism.

ဏဂ

Q: Besides cultivating our own minds while walking, standing, sitting, and lying down, and to correct our bad habits, what Sutras should we recite?

A: Start with the Shurangama Sutra.

Q: The Shurangama Sutra is so profound that I only know how to read it, but I don't quite understand it.

A: Read it every day and you will eventually understand it one day.

৪০৫৪

Q: The Earth Store Sutra has many ghosts and spirits. I don't dare to recite it.

A: Ghosts and spirits are Bodhisattvas manifested. What is there to be afraid of? Do you have ghosts in your heart?

৪০৫৪

Q: In which destiny was I, in my last incarnation?

A: The Vajra Sutra says, "What is in the past cannot be attained." As long as you do more good deeds, recite the Buddha's name more, everything will naturally be peaceful. Major disasters will turn into minor disasters; minor disasters will turn into no disasters.

ಬೃಂಡ

Q: Why do the Buddha images have to be adorned?

A: Because when sentient beings see adorned Buddha images, they will feel respectful and will be inspired to make the resolve to attain Bodhi.

ಬೃಂಡ

Q: Why do we need so many monasteries?

A: There will be many Buddhists in the future.

We will not have enough monasteries to serve them.

୫୦୯୫

Q: Can anyone make the resolution to save the deceased in the ten Dharma Realms or will this be effective only if done by enlightened, virtuous Sanghans?

A: Of course virtuous Sanghans who are enlightened can do this, but everyone can save the deceased in the Ten Dharma Realms too. By being a good person, you are saving the deceased.

୫୦୯୫

Q: Of what use is it to bow to Buddha statues made of wood?

A: Buddha statues are not the Buddhas; the Buddhas are everyone. There's not one spot that the Dharma body of Buddhas fails to reach. Wooden statues are figures representing the significance of Buddhas in the same way that citizens salute their national flag though it is a piece of fabric or canvas. What is the use of saluting them?

∞

Q: How can a mote of dust contain a three-fold great-thousand world system?

A: You should know why a three-fold great-thousand world system cannot be contained in a mote of dust. If you understand that principle, you would understand how they can be contained therein. The Avatamsaka is just this inconceivable!

∞

Q: How do the results different for those who practice asceticism, scholarship, and the propagation of Dharma?

A: By sowing melons, we reap melons; by sowing beans, we reap beans. as is the cause, so is the effect.

ⴄⳁⳋⳆ

Q: What are the advantages to reciting Sutras?

A: There's not much advantage to reciting Sutras. It takes a lot of energy, time and effort. Your question is foolish, so my first answer is chiding. In fact, the advantages that you can see are not real. Anything that has a characteristic is illusory and false. Any tangible advantage cannot be a plus. What are intangible advantages? Every time you recite a Sutra, you cleanse your self-nature and enhance your wisdom. What is invisible to the eye is honest advantage. Superficialities are visible. This is an explanation for the importance of Sutra recitations.

ⴄⳁⳋⳆ

Q: Chinese monasteries do a ritual for feeding ghosts and spirits, called "Releases at Mt. Meng." What is it?

A: Great Master the Sixth Patriarch told Hui Ming to go and stay at Mt. Meng in Yuan

Province. Instead of going immediately, Hui Ming went three years later. There, he met a ghost who used to be a scholar in the ranks of today's Ph.D. Despite having become a ghost, he continued to create poems. He wrote a poem after seeing Great Master Hui Ming, which says:

> *Dreams are long here in this wild*
> *and forlorn desolation.*
> *I have become too languid to care about*
> *success or failure, about past and present,*
> *Or how many bunches of grass I have pulled*
> *and bouquets of flowers I have picked.*
> *The bitter rain and the biting wind*
> *almost break my heart.*
> *I flit in and out with the fireflies during*
> *the dark of the night.*
> *My shadow of a form I hide*
> *when cocks crow at first light.*
> *My only regret is not having cultivated*
> *the mind-ground from the start.*
> *Hence my fall into the realm of phantoms.*
> *Oh, the tears roll down my face.*

Great Master Hui Ming heard the ghost sing this poem and explained Dharma for him. The former scholar was saved as a result and became reborn in a higher incarnation. This is how "Releases at Mt. Meng" came about. Releases at Mt. Meng are about saving ghosts.

৪৩৫৪

Q: The Saha World is a polluted land; a world in the Flower Treasury is a pure land. The Buddha spoke the Avatamsaka Sutra in a Flower Treasury world. Does this mean that the Buddha left the Saha World and went to a Flower Treasury world?

A: He didn't leave; he's still in the Saha World. Saha is Flower Treasury, and Flower Treasury is Saha. This is a mixture of impurity and purity, a state that is neither pure nor impure.

৪৩৫৪

Q: What are the Flower Treasury Worlds?

A: They are called worlds of the Flower Treasury because they arose from the great lotus in the Sea of Perfume. The flower contains worlds as many as motes of dust. There are twenty layers to each world. Each layer has infinite worlds. The Saha World on which we live is on the thirteenth layer.

಄಄಄

Q: Can insentient beings restore their spiritual nature?

A: Yes, if they were to meet the right people who speak Dharma for them. Just as "When the Honorable Shen spoke Dharma, obdurate rocks nodded, too." They could restore their spiritual sense only if they were to meet a sage or an arhat.

಄಄಄

Q: *By Venerable Master:* What heirloom do we own?

A: We own an heirloom that is the true mind. It is the wondrous and enlightened nature of understanding that always dwells in the Tathagatha's Treasury. It's not the visible and tangible world of gold, silver, and gems.

ಐೞಚಿ

Q: Master, what should I do? My grandson died.

A: Why do you still react this way despite having studied Buddhism? Birth and death are the same!

Buddhist Terms

Q: Is there really a Dharma Ending Age?

A: If you think the Dharma will come to an end, it will. If you don't want the Dharma to end, then you are in the Proper Dharma Age.

৺৩

Q: What kind of resolve for Bodhi is considered solid?

A: The kind where we vow to cultivate the Way, regardless of what hindrances we may encounter and no matter how hard it is. We will not ever change our past vows. We will not change our minds or beliefs. We will act in accord with conditions but not change, and we will not change yet accord with conditions. Despite the circumstances, be they excellent or poor, our resolve for Bodhi shall remain firm.

৺৩

Q: Many words in Buddhist Sutras are Sanskrit transliterations. Is it more accurate to pronounce them using the Taiwanese or Mandarin dialect?

A: If you were to picture me in terms of form or to pursue me with sounds, you would be practicing in a deviant way and so could not see the Thus Come One.

୨୦୯୫

Q: It is said that the recitation of the "Six-Syllable True Words" brings boundless merit and virtue, including that Bodhisattvas of the Seventh Ground inhabit our person. What does that mean?

A: The recitation of the "Six-Syllable True Words" is not the only way to obtain boundless merit and virtue. One can also obtain them by not being greedy, not seeking, not being selfish, not pursuing personal advantage and not lying. Even though these actions will bring us merit and virtue, we should not be attached to them.

୨୦୯୫

Q: How do we detach ourselves from the mark of form?

A: Do not banter the teachings about. Do not be all talk and no action.

☙❧

Q: Why do some Buddhist scholars say that the Shurangama Sutra is false?

A: Because what this Sutra says is so true. It describes people's faults all too clearly, thus forcing demons and ghosts out of their hiding places and revealing their original form. They have to say that the Shurangama Sutra is fabricated because, first of all, they can't say it's true; second, they are unable to observe the four clear and unalterable instructions on purity, and lastly, they can't cultivate the 25 perfect penetrations.

☙❧

Q: What is Buddha?

A: Nothing at all.

৪৩৪৩

Q: How do we transcend the three realms and become liberated?

A: When you are not in the three realms, you have transcended them.

৪৩৪৩

Q: During the Venerable Master's talk, you mentioned the coming of Maitreya Buddha to this Saha world. Approximately how long will it be before he gets here?

A: It is too long for me to count.

৪৩৪৩

Q: Are arhats' segmented births and deaths temporary or permanent? Is the enlightenment realized by preeminent Sanghas of the past the same as that by Pratyekabuddhas and Arhats?

A: Have you ended your segmented birth and death? I don't know the answer to this at all, as I am neither an Arhat nor a sage.

ಬಂಛ

Q: Many people say this is the Dharma-ending Age. Is there an exact period of time for it? For example, what year during B.C.E. did it start?

A: Who knows so much? Your questions have reached the limits of my wisdom. However, you should know that, "People know whether the water is warm or cold by drinking it."

ಬಂಛ

Q: How do I start to recite, memorize, and understand the three Sutras of Shurangama, Flower Adornment, and Dharma Flower? With which Sutra should I start first?

A: You can start with any of these Sutras. Their Dharma is equal; there's no better or worse. If you think to make a choice, then you are having idle thoughts and essentially you don't understand these Buddhist Sutras. Learn the Sutra that you want to learn. There's no particular order.

ಸಿಂಶ

Q: What are precepts?

A: Precepts are about the principles of no fighting, no greed, no seeking, no selfishness, no pursuing personal advantage, and no lying. Don't go looking for precepts in precept handbooks. It is something everyone can do and can practice.

ಸಿಂಶ

Q: The Buddhist scriptures say that the contemplation of sound is the best for attaining enlightenment. The perfection of the ear organ is the most effective method to enlightenment. However, I believe our eyes are the most valuable among all the sense organs; our ears come next. In my opinion, our eyes ought to be the most effective organ to attaining enlightenment, not our ears.

A: Actually, every one of our sense organs is the best. There are no seconds. Whatever resonates is number one; what doesn't click is number two.

৪৩

Q: What is the use of reciting the 42 Avatamsaka Syllabary?

A: The Syllabary has a limitless amount of wonderful functions. It can eradicate all our karmic obstacles. Its power is inconceivable and indescribable.

৪৩

Q: What is a "vehicle," and how do the Great Vehicle and Small Vehicle differ?

A: A "vehicle" provides transport for passengers. A great vehicle can seat more passengers and a smaller vehicle fewer. Since beings' faculties, nature, and tendencies are different, their inclination toward either the great or the small vehicle are different too. In reality, both the Mahayana and the Theravada are one. Don't discriminate here.

၈ဢ

Q: Buddhism divided into the traditions of the North and South. What is your view on this?

A: Buddhist principles are essentially no different within the various schools and sects. The northern and southern traditions were established only because later generations lost the truth. They tried to counter each other. Why do we slay those of our own kind? The Great Vehicle claims that the Small Vehicle is too small; the Small Vehicle does not respect those of the Great Vehicle. Actually, anyone who tries to create schisms in Buddhism is no Buddhist. There's no need to mention the Great Vehicle or the Small Vehicle, there's not a single vehicle!

The cause of war is selfishness and self-interest. Wishing to harm others and benefit ourselves, we only know to praise ourselves   and slander others.

୨୦୯ଷ

Q: Aren't arhats able to become liberated from birth and death?

A: They only take care of themselves.

୨୦୯ଷ

Q: Shakyamuni Buddha cultivated for three great eons before he became a Buddha. Is this length of time fixed?

A: Have you heard of Dhyana Master Gao Fongmiao? The one who sat at Xitianmu (Eye of Western Heaven), where the cliff was shaped like an inverted lotus. He fell over the cliff when he dozed off, but Weitou Bodhisattva saved him and carried him up back up.

Q: I've heard of him.

A: You've heard about that incident. Well, what happened to him ought to answer your question.

ଚୌଔ

Q: What exactly is "Dharma"?

A: Dharma means energy, energy that can penetrate heaven and earth. All Buddhas and Bodhisattvas and we are one because our energies are connected.

ଚୌଔ

Q: We talk about how arhats and Bodhisattvas are different and similar. Will the Venerable Master please explain the differences between arhats and Bodhisattvas for us?

A: "Arhats" and "Bodhisattvas" are just terms. This is a matter of difference between people. Bodhisattvas benefit other people while arhats only cultivate for themselves. These are stages of cultivation. As ordinary people, we don't understand the states of arhats. As we go back and forth, deducing and imagining, we will have wasted all our time.

∞

Q: The "Incense Praise" has this in its lyrics: "Our sincere intention thus fulfilling as all Buddhas now show their perfect body." Some books say that all Buddhas show their golden body. Is it their perfect body or their golden body?

A: The golden body is the perfect body; the perfect body is the golden body.

∞

Q: Will the Venerable Master please explain samadhi?

A: "Samadhi" is a Sanskrit word that means proper concentration and proper reception. Note that proper is the opposite of deviant.

ഇരുള

Q: A Dharma Master thinks that "Thus I have heard" in the Sutras should be changed to "Thus I have translated." I wonder which phrase is right?

A: To tell you the truth, neither one is right. When the Venerable Ananda compiled the Sutras, he added "Thus I have heard" to the beginning of Sutras to prove that he had personally heard the Buddha say these words. This particular phrase wasn't said by the Buddha. If you use "Thus I have translated," you don't even understand what this is supposed to mean. Ananda only compiled the scriptures; he didn't translate them.

ഇരുള

Q: 1. According to Theravadan teachings, the soul between skandhas is reborn instantly. But Mahayana Sutras say that it is reborn after seven to 49 days.

2. Where did humans come from? How come there are so many people?

A: 1. There's no specific length of time that the soul between skandhas lasts. Some don't become reborn until after several great aeons. Some will become reborn immediately.

2. People don't necessarily reincarnate to become people again. Some become chickens, some become dogs, or other animals. According to the various individual karmas and retributions, living beings are separated into those born from the womb, from eggs, from moisture, and from transformation. They go from one type to another just like people can go to Belgium all of sudden, and go from Belgium to China all of a sudden. Nothing remains static. Anyway, knowing these things don't necessarily help cultivation.

೩೦೮೩

Q: The Buddhist Sutras say, "The Buddha is

our self-nature. Everyone can become a Buddha." Will the Venerable Master please explain why we're Buddhas and yet not Buddhas, and why we always bow to the Buddha images?

A: Most people think this line refers to our physical body being the same as that of Buddhas. But we're not talking about the body, but our inherent nature. If we want to become a Buddha, we must cultivate to understand this principle. This line means that we have to have a certain understanding to become a Buddha; it doesn't mean that one is already a Buddha. For instance, we don't get a Ph.D. just because we want it. To get our doctorate degree, we must finish elementary school, high school, university, and then a doctorate program. Just because I say I'm a Buddha, it doesn't mean that I am a Buddha. If that were the case, then I could just call myself an emperor and I would become an emperor. It doesn't work that way.

Q: Will the Venerable Master please explain what Buddhism means by the purity of the six senses?

A: "The purity of the six senses" means: the eyes are unaffected by forms; the ears are unaffected by sounds; the nose is unaffected by scents; the tongue is unaffected by flavors; the body is unaffected by sensation; and the mind is unaffected by doctrines. Being unaffected by states is "samadhi," which is concentration. Concentration doesn't occur only in sitting meditation, necessarily. Samadhi can occur while walking, standing, sitting, and reclining.

ဆာက

Q: Our bodies must be pure so that we'll have sharira.

A: Right. You should stay single and not touch women. Having been intimate with a woman, whatever sharira you may have will only be glass.

Q: The Buddhist scriptures often talk about the shakings of the great earth. Why do earthquakes happen?

A: Earthquakes can also be called people-quakes because people are connected to earthquakes. When people quake, the earth also quakes. If people were not to quake, then the earth would not quake either. Why did the earth quake in six ways when the Buddha entered Nirvana? It is because people panicked and were awfully scared, so their seven emotions and six desires seeped out, causing the earth to quake.

ଯୁତ୍ତ

Q: What does "affliction is Bodhi" mean?

A: If you don't know, how could you have become even more distraught than you had been? There's not much to get out of this. It's not at all difficult to understand. It's as easy as flipping over the palm of your hand. Affliction is one side of the coin while Bodhi is on the other side. This, too, is just like ice and water.

ഇരുങ്ങ

Q: The Heart Sutra has this passage, "Form is emptiness and emptiness is form." Is this talking about women or men? It's not necessarily an explanation of male and female forms only, right? Will the Venerable Master please explain?

A: All female and male forms are included here. True emptiness contains wonderful existence while wonderful existence contains true emptiness. True emptiness is not empty, therefore, it is wonderful existence. Wonderful existence is not existent, therefore, it is true emptiness. "Form is emptiness," is simply about not looking outside for happiness because it is actually inherent to our nature. We don't need to dwell on form. There's true happiness in emptiness. Therefore, "Form is emptiness and emptiness is form."

☙ℭ

Q: What Three Impossibilities do Buddhas have?

A: Have you read the Avatamsaka Sutra? Go back and really study it.

☙ℭ

Q: The Sutras say "To the Buddha I return and rely, vowing that all living beings understand the great Way profoundly, and bring forth the Bodhi mind. To the Dharma I return and rely, vowing that all living beings deeply enter the Sutra Treasury, and have wisdom like the sea. To the Sangha I return and rely, vowing that all living beings form together a great assembly, one and all in harmony." Since monks or nuns have to manage the great assembly, everything that they do must accord with the Buddha's way. But people are not perfect. People are still people. If they can't even uphold the rules themselves, aren't they misleading living beings by managing the great assembly?

A: There's good and evil in the world; there are those who cultivate and there are those who don't. There are those who truly support Buddhism and there are those who only use Buddhism to supply themselves with clothing and food. To the latter, Buddhism is a business. They try to fool people into believing that fish eyes are pearls. Whether people are fooled depends on whether they have the ability to select the right Dharma, the understanding of what is right and what is wrong. Without such an ability, people mistake the thief for their son, misery for joy, and black for white.

8003

Q: What is the difference between nature, consciousness, thoughts, and mind?

A: Newborns are vivacious, free from identities like others, self, living beings, and life spans. Initially, an infant is "nature." Once the baby begins to suckle, his "consciousness" is strengthened. After drinking milk, he learns to dress so that he will not be cold or embarrassed. He understands hunger, thirst, warmth, and cold. That would be "thoughts." When he is grown, he wants this and that. That would be the "mind" working. These are actually four types of mental states, but they could be said to be one too because they are inextricably connected. They all belong to the same family. Although there are four terms, their fundamental quality is the same. The offender that has created them is "karma."

Q: Why are there asuras in the three whole-some destinies if they don't belong there?

A: Although asuras belong to the three whole-some destinies, they are often dragged into the four evil destinies too. Why are they classi-fied as one of the three wholesome destinies? It is because some of them have done some good deeds, such as fighting against injustice. Their deeds cover extreme good and extreme bad. That is why sometimes they are grouped into one of the three wholesome destinies and sometimes the four evil destinies.

৪৩০৪

Q: Which realm do ghosts and spirits belong to out of the Ten Dharma Realms?

A: Ghosts and spirits don't belong to the same category. Ghosts belong to the Dharma realm of ghosts while spirits belong to the realm of spirits. Ghosts are yin in nature while spirits are yang in nature.

Q: I would like to ask the Venerable Master about sharira. Some people say they are rocks. Some people say one sharira will split into two while others say they will disappear. Will you please explain?

A: Sharira are a result of keeping to the precepts: no killing, no stealing, and primarily, no sexual activity. That way, one's precious things are not lost. What are those "precious things?" I believe every one of us knows what is the essence of life, I don't need to say too much. If we refrain from sexual activity, our sharira will naturally be bright and brilliant, more solid than diamonds. As far as what the average person says about it multiplying... I have never experimented with them or done tests on sharira before. I can only tell you this: by keeping the precepts, one will have sharira. On the other hand, if one doesn't keep the precepts, there will be no sharira.

Q & A - Buddhism Terms

෯෯

Q: The Avatamsaka Sutra says, "To the Buddha I return and rely, vowing that all living beings proliferate the seeds of Buddhism and bring forth the unsurpassed resolve." And yet when we recite the three refuges, it's been changed to "To the Buddha I return and rely, vowing that all living beings understand the great Way profoundly, and bring forth the Bodhi mind."

A: No dharma is fixed. He changed it because he thought it was easier to read, that's all!

෯෯

Q: What is the "transmission that occurs from one mind to another mind?" How does the transmission of one mind to another occur?

A: The transmission of Dharmas occurs often. The amount that you receive is yours. No one sees this transmission and no one knows who has received how much.

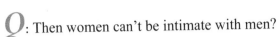

Q: Then women can't be intimate with men?

A: Right! That's right too. That's why Buddhist monasticism doesn't allow monks or nuns to marry; instead they watch and encourage each other to avoid promiscuity. To be sexually promiscuous is to violate precepts. Cultivators must be very clear on this issue between men and women. If they're not clear about this, they would merely be pretending that fish eyes are pearls.

Q: Is actual truth "emptiness?"

A: It could also contain "existence." If you think it exists, then it exists. If you think it's empty, then it's empty. Emptiness does not obstruct the mundane, while the mundane does not obstruct actuality. Wonderful existence is contained in true emptiness, while wonderful

S
E
X

A
C
T
U
A
L

T
R
U
T
H

existence contains true emptiness. You don't want to be confused by true emptiness or misled by wonderful existence.

๛◌ผ

Q: Buddhism is separated into the two schools of the Manifest and the Secret. Which one is more helpful to living beings? Do those at the City of the Ten Thousand Buddhas study both the Manifest and the Secret schools?

A: The "Secret" in the Secret and Manifest schools is not the kind of secret we imagine. The Manifest isn't what we imagine it to be either. The Manifest School in Buddhism means that it allows everyone to understand: when I speak Dharma for person A, person B also understands; when I speak Dharma for person B, person A also understands. This is Manifest. Secret means that I speak Dharma for Smith but Lee doesn't understand that Dharma. When I speak Dharma for Lee, Smith doesn't understand. It is definitively "secret." It doesn't mean that it is secretive so that people wouldn't understand. It's not talking about Tantric practices for couples, for singles, for the confused, or for the outrageous.

ക്കരു

Q: What is the difference between consciousness-only and prajna?

A: Consciousness-only is what is known only to consciousness. Prajna is wisdom, which is unknown to consciousness.

ക്കരു

Q: What are the three kind of non-retreat?

A: The non-retreating position is a resultant position for Mahayana Bodhisattvas whereby they do not retreat to study and practice of the Two Vehicles and the Theravada teachings. The non-retreating resolve refers to one's resolve for Bodhi. One would never withdraw from cultivating enlightenment and achieving one's vows. The non-retreating conduct means that one always moves ahead boldly and cultivates vigorously, never backsliding or becoming lazy after cultivating for a while. For instance, one does not stop and turn back after cultivating for two or three days, asking, "Why haven't I become a Buddha yet?"

ༀༀༀ

Q: What's the difference between Sutras and mantras?

A: What do you think the difference is? Mantras include vows and functions for fulfilling those vows. Sutras discuss methods of cultivation that we must learn. Once you understand the principle, you must do it. In addition, the meaning in the Sutras has been translated from Sanskrit into Chinese. Mantras are not translated from Sanskrit into Chinese; only their sounds are transliterated. These are the esoteric true words of all Buddhas.

ༀༀༀ

Q: How should we go about liberating life for a deceased ancestor who in life had become mentally disabled as a result of an accident?

A: Don't be too superstitious about the ceremony to liberate life. You should act according to the golden mean: not too much and not too little. Do what you can and try your best.

༄༅༅

Q: Earlier you talked about a past disciple who had the Five Eyes and the Six Penetrations, including the penetration of no-outflow. What exactly is that? From what I understand, that means he has already certified to arhatship.

A: Precisely how do you define the penetration of no-outflow? The Five Eyes and the Six Penetrations that I talk about are not necessarily what you perceive them to be, either. There are approximate penetrations and ultimate penetrations. The person I mentioned had attained approximate penetrations, so he understood very little; he only knew, for instance, others' thoughts. Most people can reach that level. On the other hand, someone who has ultimate penetration knows not just the thoughts of one individual but the thoughts of each and every individual in the entire world. Not only does he know the thoughts of human beings, but the Thus Come One knows the thoughts of all kinds of living beings.

ഇരു

Q: Is a demon that appears during one's meditation a creation of the mind? If it is made from the mind alone, is that the same kind of demon that you talked about earlier?

A: When you have offended demons outside of you, the demons in you will also act up. There's not just one kind of demon and not just one kind of ghost. There are heavenly demons, earth demons, spiritual demons, ghostly demons, demons who are people, demons made from the mind, and demons that are created by external states. There isn't just one kind, but many kinds.

Q: Is Mt. Sumeru a material entity that really exists? Or is it a state seen during meditative concentration? Or is it just a part of the Indian philosophy?

A: Mt. Sumeru is right before your eyes. Who can you blame if you can't see it? "Everything is wrong when we are attached to forms; and yet non-doing means that we sink into the void." Let's see what you'll do.

Q: What are the three obstacles in the saying, "All evils are eradicated and the three obstacles are completely gone."

A: The three obstacles refer to the obstacle that is karma, the obstacle that is retribution, and the obstacle that is affliction. There's no form to the obstacle that is karma. It's fortunate that there's no form to it, otherwise it would burst open the trichiliocosm.

ಬಂಬ

Q: The Buddha said that the Buddha nature is pure originally. Then where did ignorance come from?

A: Ignorance was that single unenlightened thought we let happen, which in turn caused us to speculate on three subtle mental states. From those, we became caught in six coarse mental concepts which lead us to assume those states to be our conditions. Ignorance comes from emotions and love. Ignorance is an alias for delusion.

ಬಂಬ

Q: Please clarify the relationship between the external Triple Jewel (Buddha, Dharma, and Sangha) and the internal triple jewel (essence, breath, and spirit).

A: The spirit is parallel to the Buddha, essence is parallel to the Sangha, and breath is parallel to the Dharma. The internal Triple Jewel is the

Dharma body and wisdom life of people while the external Triple Jewel are role models for people. While we are protecting and supporting the external Triple Jewel, we should also take care of our essence, breath, and spirit. Be chaste so that we don't expend any of the internal Triple Jewel. Sangha doesn't simply refer to people who have left the householder's life. Ultimately the term refers to those who don't waste their essence and energy. Laypeople who don't waste their essence and breath are Sangha members, too, believe it or not!

Q: What is the Vajra Bodhi Sea?

A: What is Vajra? It means indestructibility. What is the Sea of Bodhi? It is the sea of great enlightenment. Actually, the Vajra Bodhi Sea is deeper and wider than any ocean.

Q: "If people wish to know all Buddhas throughout the three periods of time, they should contemplate the nature of the Dharma Realm and that the Thus Come Ones are made from the mind alone." What shape is this mind?

A: It's shapeless. The mind is just the mind. If it were to have any shape, it wouldn't be the mind. We're not talking about that gray matter that's our brain; we're talking about the real mind, which is omnipresent, pervading all of space and the Dharma Realm. If we recognize this, we will have reached the true mind completely.

ৼজ

Q: What is bliss? What is soul? How do we make contact with our soul?

A: I've already talked about what is bliss. Not fighting is bliss. Not being greedy is bliss. Not being selfish, not pursuing personal advantage, and not lying are bliss. When you're fighting, you expend a lot of effort and brainpower thinking about how to fight people, which will make you quite miserable. When you're greedy, you can't sleep at night and the food tastes bland to you. That's misery. When you search for things outside, including men pursuing women and women pursuing men, you forget everything. You don't even care about your parents; you only know to go after the object of your affection. That's misery. Being selfish, you always do things that hurt others and help yourself. Pursuing self-advantage means that you only know about benefiting yourself but not others. Lying is misery too. Being discontent is misery. Being content is bliss. I've already said that earlier. The soul is your Buddha nature. To most people, the Buddha nature is the soul. It can become a Buddha if you cultivate well. If you don't cultivate, then it becomes a ghost. You want to make contact with your soul, but you can't see your soul. To see it, you have to cultivate spiritually and sever your desires and love. You cannot possibly know what your soul

is like if you don't sever desire and love as you cultivate the spiritual path.

୨୦୯୫

Q: What is Right Samadhi in cultivation? What kind of a state is that?

A: Right Samadhi is a state of deep absorption during which one has no deviant views. There's no Right Samadhi if one has deviant views. The Shurangama Sutra says so clearly; "It is a wholesome state if one doesn't consider oneself a sage because of that state; if one does consider oneself a sage, one will fall into the deviant hoards." This is an explanation of Right Samadhi, and the best explanation at that.

୨୦୯୫

Q: Could the Venerable Master please talk about the third eye?

A: There are Five Eyes. Not just three.

Q: What is the Dharma of causes and conditions?

A: The Dharma spoken by causes and conditions, I say is just emptiness, which is also called false by name, as well the meaning of the Middle Way.

ಬಙಿ

Q: What kind of compassion is great compassion based on the knowledge that we are all the same?

A: Feeling that we're in pain when we see others in pain, we would want to alleviate their pain in any way possible. We would treat others the way we treat ourselves. One is all and all is one. This is great compassion based on the understanding that we're the same.

ಬಙಿ

C
O
M
P
A
S
S
I
O
N

Q: The Shurangama Sutra says that because living beings don't know to dwell in the true mind at all times, they are mixed up and therefore revolve around the wheel of transmigration. Venerable Master, what is the true mind?

A: The true mind is the mind without any sexual desire. Anyone without sexual desire is someone no longer mixed up, someone who understands what it means to dwell in the true mind at all times.

ಬಿಂಜ

Q: What is Wonderful Dharma Lotus Flower Sutra?

A: It's the most wonderful Sutra among all Sutras. We shouldn't miss the opportunity to attain wondrousness. It wouldn't be wonderful if we failed to receive any wondrousness. No one should be devoid of wondrousness; everyone should go and find this "wondrousness." But first, you must bear the pain and withstand the toil, work hard on studying this wonderful Dharma.

ॐ

Q: Is there one absolute truth, or is there none?

A: Everything is relative; there are no absolutes. There is one thing that is the absolute truth: that even this absolute doesn't exist. Even the "one" is gone. Once you understand the one absolute, you cannot become attached to this absolute. Attachment to the absolute, the truth, is still a form of attachment; consequently, that absolute truth will be of no use to you. You must let go of that absolute too. As it is said, "The myriad Dharmas return to one, and to where does that one return?" To where should "one" go back? There's not even that "one". If there's not a thing, what might that be? That's "zero." Zero creates the heavens, earth, and myriad things; it creates immortals, Buddhas, and sages. They are all born from this zero. That zero is limitless and boundless. Think about this number. If you put a "0" next to a "1 ," you've got "10", add another circle, it's a hundred. Draw another circle and it's one thousand. Draw yet another zero, and you have ten thousand, then thousands upon thousands, and tens of thousands upon tens of thousands. There's no end to the number of zeros that you could draw. Even the computer can't compute that figure. You say, "That's a number." You have to let go of that "a" then. What is there if there is nothing? A zero is not a number; being zero, it is nothing. So this "one", this absolute of yours basically doesn't exist.

The Buddha is just the fundamental nature in every one of us. "All living beings have the Buddha nature; all are capable of becoming Buddhas." So, to be able to become Buddhas is most democratic. Anyone can become a Buddha!

৪৩৫৪

Q: How do you explain, "The sentient and insentient together perfect the wisdom of all modes"?

A: The sentient and insentient refer to beings with blood and breath and beings that lack blood and breath. What are insentient beings? They're plants. Plants have their nature of life but not any emotion. "Together perfect the wisdom of all modes" means that all of them will realize Buddhahood. No computer can figure out who will realize Buddhahood first or last.

৪০৫৪

Q: What is the Mark of Longevity (the attribute of having a lifespan)?

A: Wanting to live forever.

৪০৫৪

Q: What is great compassion?

A: Forgiveness for others. No matter what it is that other people have done, we consider ourselves to have been in the wrong. To be able to forgive others, not see their faults, and allow them to change—that is great compassion.

ഇരുജ

Q: What are mantras?

A: Mantras are just honest words. If you were honest, then everything you say become effective mantras because ghosts and spirits obey them. Mantras are "true words," which means the truth.

ഇരുജ

Q: What is Bodhi?

A: Bodhi means not picking anything up. Let it all go! "It" includes money, sex, fame, food, and sleep.

ഇരുജ

Q: I still don't understand the nature of living beings. Also, what is the Buddha nature?

A: It's the Buddha nature once you have become enlightened; it's the nature of living beings while you are deluded.

ഇൽ

Q: What kinds of things are wonderful?

A: The wonderful Dharma is wonderful. What is wonderful? Living beings are wonderful. What else is wonderful? Buddhas are wonderful too. What else is wonderful? Everything in the universe is wonderful. Everything is the wonderful Dharma.

ഇൽ

Q: How do you explain that the day we are born is the day that we die? Is it that we die as soon as we are born?

A: That's right. We're dead as soon as we are

born; but it's not that our life ends, it's that the 84,000 pores in our body die. From our birth-day onward, one pore dies each day until most of us reach age 60 to 100. Our pores become clogged because of dead tissue though new cells development. In any case, nothing is born on our birthday and nothing is dead on our day of passing.

૪૦૯૪

Q: But if we clear away all those worlds that are as numerous as motes of dust, does that mean there would be no more worlds?

A: To clear away those worlds means that evil worlds filled with the five turbidities are gone; however, wholesome and pure worlds as many as motes of dust remain.

૪૦૯૪

Q: What exactly is the "Wordless Sutra"?

A: It is "not giving rise to a single thought."

If you do not give rise to a single thought, everything naturally returns to still emptiness. That's all that the Buddhadharma is about; there's nothing else.

৪৩৫৪

Q: What is true giving?

A: It's to give up what we cannot give up. That's true giving.

৪৩৫৪

Q: What is "great kindness despite a lack of affinities"?

A: It means that we try to save those with whom we have no affinities. By being kind to those who are unkind to us, we are acting out of great kindness despite having no affinities.

৪৩৫৪

Q: What is the power of samadhi?

A: It is the ability to not be turned by situations, but to turn situations around. If you can turn situations around, you are no different than the Thus Come One.

৪০০৪

Q: What is the true self?

A: It's our inherent nature that realizes Buddhahood. Once we have realized Buddhahood, it's the true self. Before we have realized Buddhahood, it's all false.

৪০০৪

Q: We talk about different worlds as many as motes of dust in Buddhalands. What's the use of having heard the names of so many worlds?

A: I'll tell you, this is a state according to the Avatamsaka Sutra. It teaches us to expand our minds.

৪০০৪

Q: What is the straightforward mind?

A: It's said that, "The straightforward mind is the Bodhimanda." If we were not straightforward, we would not have come to a place of cultivation. With a mind that is straight, we reach the Bodhimanda quickly. We're not talking about a place of cultivation such as the facility in which we're lecturing the Sutras now, but the Bodhimanda that is Buddhahood. The straightforward and right mind is not crooked and twisted. What does it mean to be crooked and twisted? It means to be sycophantic.

ॐ

Q: Why is it said that the Buddha neither comes nor goes?

A: Because the Buddha's Dharma body pervades all of space and the Dharma Realm. He is everywhere present and nonexistent.

ॐ

Q: Typically, our first thought at the sight of good food is to eat it and our first thought at the sight of pretty things is to own them. Is that the Primary Truth?

A: No, don't get confused. The so-called "first thought" is the revelation of your true mind, or your original face. It is view and knowledge at its most fundamental. Thoughts of greed for food, for nice things belong to the false mind, the mind of greed, and not the true mind.

෨൦൬ඃ

Q: What is the mind?

A: The mind is the Dharma Realm. Your mind is bigger than all of empty space, bigger than the universe. It's just that you don't use it.

෨൦൬ඃ

Q: What is the Vajra Samadhi?

A: The Vajra Samadhi is a state of mind that is eternal and unchanging.

୫୦୧୫

Q: How large is this Sutra?

A: It fills up three thousand great world systems of a thousand worlds.

Q: Why is it so large?

A: Because there are so many dust particles.

Q: Would the Sutra be smaller if there were fewer dust particles? Where would a larger Sutra be?

A: It's not that the Sutra is large but that it exists in every mote of dust. The number of dust motes is large. Not only is the total number of dust motes large, but the worlds are large too; so this Sutra can become really huge as well. Where is this Sutra? That's a meditation topic (koan). It's wherever you say it is.

❧☙

Q: Do human beings have souls?

A: Of course. Buddhists believe in souls. If you don't believe in souls, you don't understand Buddhism.

❧☙

Q: What is the meaning of life?

A: Death.

❧☙

Q: What is wisdom?

A: Wisdom is about always knowing the right thing to do and say.

❧☙

Q: What are souls?

A: Souls are ghosts. Having cultivated successfully, they become Buddhas; not having cultivated, they are ghosts.

ଅଔଷ

Q: Where is the soul?

A: It's in this jail-like body of ours when we're alive. Once we've successfully cultivated, it leaves this jail cell and attains true freedom.

ଅଔଷ

Q: What are false thoughts?

A: This question on what are false thoughts is a false thought.

ଅଔଷ

Q: What is true emptiness?

A: Zero.

ଅଔଷ

Q: What is the destiny of animals about?

A: Acting on one's ignorance and deviant views, one eventually becomes an animal.

৪০০৪

Q: What is the "first thought"?

A: It's that very first thought of understanding before you consciously deliberate. Whenever you think, you are using your human brain and not your enlightened mind.

৪০০৪

Q: Do King Yama and the Ghost of Impermanence exist?

A: That depends on whether you can avoid death. If you can avoid death, there is no Ghost of Impermanence. If you're certain that you will not have to undergo any retribution, there is no King Yama.

৪০০৪

Q: What is liberation?

A: It's to attain true freedom, to be free from hindrances and bindings, and to come and go as we please.

৪০৩

While his disciples were translating the Shurangama Sutra, they asked the Venerable Master about the meaning of many words in the Sutra text.

Venerable Master (after explaining those words): You have to understand that the translation of the Shurangama Sutra into Chinese utilizes many different terms for one meaning. That translation avoids repetition of the same words and keeps the text elegant throughout. You must pay attention to this, too, when you're translating this Sutra into English.

৪০৩

Q: Is the Middle Way the state of neither existence nor non-existence?

A: The Middle Way is not "neither existence nor non-existence." It embodies existence and emptiness; and yet it does not fall for existence or emptiness. To fall for existence means that one leans too heavily toward existence; to fall for emptiness means that one leans too heavily toward emptiness. The Middle Way is about being unattached to existence and emptiness. Of course, if you are searching for the Middle Way, you are attached to the Middle Way, which would not be the Middle Way.

Social Issues

Q: Will the future savior of China be a Buddhist?

A: Since he will be a savior, he will be considered Buddhist even though he may not be. The reason is that he will relieve the suffering of humankind and will help people attain bliss. If he were not a real savior, he would not be a Buddhist even though he might call himself one.

               ཚ◌ঙ

Q: This country is over-populated. Does the present birth control policy violate the law of cause and effect?

A: Being over-populated is the same as being under-populated. I think a national policy such as "one child only" is wrong. Since each family can only have one child, eventually everyone will be male. How can a country of only men and no women procreate? This policy will mean the extinction of a country and the human race in the future. To really manage a country well, [the government] should allow each couple to have two babies. Two kids can keep each other company and they can be a boy and a girl. If they were both males, one can be exchanged for a female from a family with only female babies, and vice versa. It is perfectly all right and legal to adopt a son-in-law into the family. However, if people were to have too many babies the way pigs give birth to litters of piglets, people would experience a shortage of food.

ಬಾಣ

Q: What is the reason for the war in the Middle East?

A: Reincarnated asuras insist on killing and setting fires.

ಬಾಣ

Q: Why are there so many earthquakes nowadays?

A: Because people have bad tempers.

ೞೞ

Q: How do wars come about?

A: Wars occur because we are violent within. Wars occur because our minds are not at peace.

ೞೞ

Q: How do we stop warfare?

A: Being gentle and kind is the most fundamental solution to the ending of warfare.

ೞೞ

Q: Will children of divorced parents become successes?

A: Excellent question! Don't you see that there are children with problems everywhere? Their parents are to be blamed for not being responsible enough to teach and discipline their offspring. Children become wayward because there's no coordination between education at home and education at school. Both sides have failed. Young people are so controlled by television and computer that they lose their freedom. Freedom is widely touted in the Western society; but in my view, this type of freedom is superstitious, misconstrued, unreasonable, and totally not free.

Q: Most people say, for good fengshui (geomancy), we should: hang a mirror at the front door, have green plants on the left side of the room, hang two swords above the owner's bed, and hang wind chimes along the hall ways. Is it so?

A: 1. Mirrors symbolize purity, implying that as we leave our residence we are physically pure. The mirror is said to purify in much the same way a broom is used to sweep the floor to remove dirt. Mirrors also symbolize clarity, the idea being that we become clear about phenomena and noumena. With that clarity, we are content to accept life as it is, and are free from greed and seeking. That's the fengshui principle behind installing mirrors. Unfortunately, most ignorant people believe in diabolical ideas, thinking that demons won't dare to invade their homes by installing mirrors that reflect demons. Simply by thinking in this way, demons have already taken a hold of them.

2. Foliage are just decorations.

3. The sword of wisdom slashes away emotional ties. But one needs to have self-control. Otherwise, a man and a woman may each end up with a sword in hand as they challenge each other. Demons may not have appeared if we had not hung those swords. But once we have hung them up, demons come to challenge you. You never know who will win or lose.

4. Wind chimes symbolize the process of withering away, meaning that the family will be on the decline, wilting away by the day.

Anyhow, fengshui actually comes from our minds. By being kind, open and honest, we will find that things work out for the best. Even negatives will become positives. When we are unkind, everything will turn out poorly; even positives will become negatives. That is why the Buddha said, "Everything is made from the mind alone." Those of old in China said, "Everyone believes that the excellent grave site is in the mountains. Little do they know that the best site is that square inch that is their mind." Street quacks argue forcefully and unreasonably, developing incorrect theories to fool ignorant men and women. What a pity! What a pity!

Q: The phenomena of homosexuality and unwed mothers are causes for concern. How should parents educate their children and themselves in the midst of such social disorder?

A: This is a very good question. The reason that society now faces these issues is because "Fathers do not act like fathers and mothers do not act like mothers." Nowadays parents have children because they enjoy sex, not because they consider children important. They only know how to make babies, but not how to teach them. Couples divorce on a whim, whereupon children become fatherless and motherless. The real cause of these problems is that married couples don't know how to be married and parents don't know how to parent. The world would be free of these problems if parents would educate their children by following the example of Mencius' mother. She moved three times to find an environment suitable for her son's education.

৪০০৪

Q: Our parents gave us our bodies. But should I be filial though they were cruel to me when I was young?

A: "The more they love you, the more they criticize you." Both of them hoped that you would become a success. They were afraid that you would take the wrong path.

৪০০৪

Q: Why are women underprivileged?

A: Who says women are underprivileged? The men in this world love women.

৪০৪৪

Q: What should we do if others libel us when we try to serve our community?

A: Work even harder if people libel you when you work for the community. It's not really genuine service if you were to stop it because of libel.

৪০৪৪

Q: How do we improve our relationships with people, especially not having others talk behind our backs at the workplace?

A: If you didn't do anything bad, then the person who talks behind your back is wrong. But if you did do something bad so that it's a juicy topic for gossip, then the more they talk about you, the more you deserve it.

ജഇ

Q: Dharma Master, what do you think of this prediction: the human race will become extinct as a result of a major disaster at the end of this century or the beginning of the next century?

A: Well, the best would be not to come back in the next century. Why are you bothering with this? You may remember the events of this century, but you will forget them by the time you are born in the next century. For instance, you remembered to ask this question now, but you will forget what you know in the next century. How is that useful?

ജഇ

Q: The number of calamities in the world is on the rise. How do we eradicate them to help others and ourselves?

A: There would be no calamities if we were to not get mad, not fight, and not cheat and not hurt each other.

৪৩৫৪

Q: Why are there poor people?

A: Poor people do not have blessings in this life because in their previous lives they did not do good deeds to earn merit and virtue, they did not sow any roots of goodness, they always tried to take advantage of others, and they fretted over their gains and losses.

৪৩৫৪

Q: How do we help sick people?

A: You should cure your own sicknesses before you try to cure other people's sicknesses.

৪৩৫৪

Q: I heard that you recently met one of the presidential candidates in the next election. Did he ask you to predict his chances of winning the election?

A: No. I just told him to be a good president it would be appropriate for him to uphold the six ideals at the City of Ten Thousand Buddhas: no fighting, no greed, no seeking, no selfishness, no pursuing personal advantage and no lying. A good president would uphold these six principles.

೧೦೮

Q: Venerable Master, you said that China will improve after it reaches its worst. Exactly how long will that take?

A: There is no set time as it all depends on people's minds. We need to see what the Chinese people will do.

೧೦೮

Q: Given the prospect of Taiwan's future, how should we cultivate to avert our collective karma?

A: Do not do anything evil and do everything that is good.

Q: Master, did you know ahead of time about the China Airlines plane crash on October 26? How do we avoid future disasters?

A: First of all, ask yourself if you knew about it or not. If you did, others would have too. If you did not, why would you expect others to know about it?

ജ്ഞ

Q: There are two possible reasons why people insult me: 1. I insulted them in a past life and so they insult me in this life. 2. They are sowing bad causes now. How should I think about this?

A: It's okay for you to think that you are facing the consequences. You should not imagine that other people are sowing negative effects for the future. If you have that thought, you will be developing your unwholesomeness. Even if they were really sowing unwholesome causes, don't think about it that way. In so thinking you will have sown some unwholesome causes too. Therefore, this is not a good method. It's no problem if you just don't think about it.

৪৩৫৫৪

Q: I am the only one in the family who is studying Buddhism. How can I eliminate the obstacles so that the entire family become Buddhists and benefit from the Dharma?

A: Just do things sincerely and they will naturally be moved to change.

৪৩৫৫৪

Q: Venerable Master, could you provide some instructions for your disciples?

A: For peace a country and the world to maintain peace, we must have a foundation of decency between men and women. How can the world be at peace if husbands, wives, and children do not act their parts? I beseech husbands and wives to live up to their responsibilities, take good care of their children, and do not divorce. Once we have harmony in our families, there will be peace in the land where we live. Furthermore, I must ask you not to have abortions. Just think, so many unborn babies become angered souls. So many little ghosts everywhere are seeking opportunities to return to life. Consequently, how can a society be peaceful? These baby ghosts are hard to deal with and only virtuous people who are not greedy for money can liberate them. How can societies be peaceful when karmic offenses are being committed everywhere?

ഇൗരു

Q: As an overseas Chinese, I often want to help China but find myself helpless. Please tell me what I can do for my fellow citizens in China.

A: You should try your best to do good deeds. You should not be narrow-minded and think only about helping Chinese people or certain individuals. You should help anyone who experiences hardship and difficulties. More importantly, do not get upset. You are helping China by being a good person and by changing your behavior. Since you are Chinese, your good behavior will add to China's integrity.

~ こ

Q: Someone told me that my younger brother is a jinx to my mother. He will be a threat to her life and that he should not live under the same roof as my mother. Is there a way to solve this problem?

A: I don't understand these problems, as I am a monk, not a street quack.

~ こ

Q: My husband is having an extramarital affair. What should I do?

A: Recite the Heart Sutra more often.

~ こ

Q: No more desire means no more trouble. How would this world advance if there were no more desires? What would the impetus be for scientific investigation and technological inventions. How do we control desire?

A: It is okay to invent things that help others but not the other way around. We are often remiss about what is beneficial and what is harmful. To invent things blindly creates suffering. For example, the pursuit of scientific invention has poisoned people and made them numb. What good is this type of invention?

ଷୠଓଷ

Q: How should I help others?

A: Quietly help from behind the scenes.

ଷୠଓଷ

Q: How do people who work in the area of law save others?

A: They must be fair, incorruptible, and accept no bribes as they serve the public.

෨෬

Q: Master, some single mothers have been the cause of a lot of social issues, such as abortion... I don't know whether the Master has any views or recommendations on these questions.

A: Most young people today enjoy dancing, movies, and singing. They enjoy eating, drinking, and being merry; therefore they lose their humane nature. Having lost their capacity to be humane, they don't even know they're human beings. People should be doing human-like things, but they just do ghost-like things, being secretive and violating the rules. They want to try it before marriage. As a result, children are born out of wedlock.

෨෬

Q: In a family, how should husband and wife relate? What kind of human relations are proper?

A: Husbands and wives should regard one another with respect. Children born from couples like this have the potential to become national leaders. Children of couples who do not regard each other with mutual respect have the potential to become homeless.

ഇരുഗ

Q: There are many things in this world that you won't get if you don't fight for them. But the Master talks about "no fighting, no greed, and no seeking." How should we give and take here?

A: When it is mealtime, we should eat; otherwise, we should not eat.

ഇരുഗ

Q: What is the meaning of life?

A: Hurry up and die if you feel life is meaningless. If you feel that there is meaning to your life, then that means everything.

ஐ௰

Q: The Master is so powerful. Could you help the people of China who are still suffering?

A: Once they've suffered enough, there will be no more suffering. Sweet rewards come after misery. To undergo suffering is to relieve one of suffering; to enjoy blessings is to end blessings. This is my philosophy: anything that reaches its extreme will reverse itself; anything that gets bad enough will turn into something good. It's okay. Whatever it is that all of us need to face, we will face it; once we've experienced it, there will be no more suffering. Don't worry. Don't worry about anything, like the sky falling down. Just do a good job studying.

ஐ௰

Q: Is it more appropriate to bury or cremate the deceased?

A: Cremation. Less space is required that way, only a tiny spot. If the dead use up too many places, the living will run out of places to live.

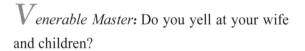

Venerable Master: Do you yell at your wife and children?

A: Yes. But sometimes when I am the one who has made a mistake, I feel good that other people yell at me too.

Venerable Master: That's not the principle here. Do you yell at people who are not related to you for no reason?

A: I do sometimes when I'm in a bad mood. Like when somebody I don't know bumps into me on the road. He should have walked with his eyes open.

Venerable Master: You should be a bit more patient there. Don't get so angry.

Q: Under such circumstances, what can we do now?

A: You should be virtuous. "No fighting, no greed, no seeking, not being selfish, no self benefiting, and no lying" are essential principles for human beings, the foundation for cultivators, and the keystone for politicians, if the latter can act according to these principles. Governments must have integrity and not take advantage of people's greed. To claim that China has no class that is rich or poor does not describe reality. In summary, remaining harmonious will benefit both sides. To act destructively will ruin both.

⊗

Q: There are many couples who don't respect each other. Does that mean their children will be failures?

A: Yes! That's why nowadays there are so many troubled children who kill and set off fires. Young children don't follow rules because they are controlled by televisions and computers.

ଚଠଔଓଷ

Q: There was a major earthquake in San Francisco. Will there be similar disasters in Taiwan in the future? How do we avoid them?

A: There will be no earthquakes if people don't get upset.

ଚଠଔଓଷ

Q: Taiwan used to be a simple place, but people have become obsessed with the lottery, stocks, etc. Everyone in Taiwan now worships money. How can this situation be improved?

A: People should learn to be dumber. They play the lottery because they're too smart. They want to get paid without having worked. They want to reap a harvest without having sowed. That is not natural.

ଚଠଔଓଷ

Q: What is life for?

A: Life is not for eating. It is to help others. Helping others is the source of happiness.

ೞೞೞ

Q: Why do my family members still dream about my father though he passed away a long time ago?

A: It is because your family members have not forgotten him.

ೞೞೞ

Q: Venerable Master, you had said that as long as you are in San Francisco, there will be no earthquakes. Now that you are away, an earthquake has taken place. What is the meaning behind it?

A: There is no meaning.

ೞೞೞ

Q: Can the law of cause and effect explain the reasons why some families have hereditary diseases?

A: Of course it can. Heredity is cause and effect. If the cause weren't planted in the past, why would they receive the same effect generation after generation?

ഇൠങ

Q: There is a lot of turmoil in our country now. What will become of this country?

A: You don't need to ask me this question as you all should know. You don't need to ask when you obviously know the answers.

When a country is about to prosper,
there will be auspicious omens.
When a country is about to become extinct,
there will be demons.
Revelations through oracles and divinations
predict the truth about situations.
Therefore we must have the foresight to know

about upcoming fortunes and disasters,
the forethought to know
what would be good and what would not.

The man who said these words, Tang Lyu, dared to kill a black cow and "report to past emperors and empresses that... I, as the emperor, am solely responsible for my people. Any mistake that my people commit is my fault." He said that his people shouldn't be blamed because he, as the leader, will take the blame. If the populace had erred any, he says to please blame him as the emperor, for he did not teach them well. He alone will be responsible. This is how ancient sages and kings were. As role models and leaders, they were courageous enough to admit their mistakes and change. They accept other people's criticisms, too.

ॐ೦ೞ

Q: Is it a good idea for Buddhists to donate their organs after they die?

A: It is better to donate their organs while they are alive and not while they're dead. What is the use of donating the organs when you won't need them anymore? There's an idiom, "Do not give to others what we don't want." True generosity means that we give what we can't bear to give away.

∞∞

Q: How do we integrate the Buddhadharma into our lives?

A: By not fighting, not being greedy, not seeking, not being selfishness, not pursuing personal advantage, and not lying.

∞∞

Q: What kind of attitude should we have about gender preferences?

A: First of all, you need to understand how people develop gender preferences. Why do they have a certain tendency? Perhaps it's because they had quarrels with their spouse. The Chinese are chauvinistic, while in America, women come first. Some Americans may say "ladies first," but not really respect women. These slogans may flatter some women, making them believe that "ladies [are] first, ladies [are] first." But the fact is that men continue to lie about this and women continue to accept the lies. This kind of "first" is a "first" without power or status. This trend makes women uncomfortable and so they do not want to marry. Men, on the other hand, became uncomfortable with overly domineering women. Hence, they wonder why they should marry.

ഇൗരു

Q: You said earlier that males are pure and women impure. Does that mean females are no good?

A: Females are the best. All men love women. Otherwise, they would never look for girlfriends to marry.

Q: What should we do with a broken family?

A: Start from scratch. Everything is a test to see what we'll do. If we don't recognize what is before our eyes, we must begin anew.

Q: Presently, there's a growing movement trying to force seniors in this country to retire.

A: "The older the ginger, the spicier it is; the older the person, the more valuable one is." Why do they all need to retire if they are in good health?

Q: How could earthquakes be avoided?

A: There will not be earthquakes if people don't get upset.

R
E
T
I
R
E
M
E
N
T

R
A
V
A
G
E
S

O
F

W
A
R

Q: Conflicts in Israel and the Middle East tell us that it's easy to make enemies but hard to unmake them. How exactly do we dissolve this kind of rivalry?

A: It has accumulated bit by bit. During this trip to Europe, I visited Poland. There, the Germans killed an incredible number of Jews [during WWII]. Each grave has tens of thousands of people in it. Tens of thousands people in one grave.

⊰⊱

Q: Is there hope for the conflicts in the Middle East?

A: There would be no war if we were kind and genial. The cause and effect that brings about war is lack of kindness.

⊰⊱

Q: What do test tube babies symbolize?

A: They are a symbol that the human race will soon become extinct!

⁪⁣⁳

Q: I heard that it's wrong to have abortions according to Buddhism. But I did so without any idea of this before, what can I do to make it up now?

A: The greatest good is but to change the mistakes that one has made. Offenses large enough to fill up the universe vanish through repentance.

⁪⁣⁳

Q: Citizens should be loyal to their country. Is there any offense for the pilots who were ordered to bomb the enemy in the Middle East? If so, what kind of attitude should they have [as they face their retribution]?

A: This question can't be cleared up even if you were to go to the international court of justice! This is an issue too huge for an average citizen like me to solve. This has to do with power of countries, individuals, and world leaders. This is not an issue that I can resolve.

⊱⊰

Q: If we cannot retaliate against someone who has humiliated us, then we should be patient according to Buddhism. But in the eyes of others, we're little wimps. What should we do, really?

A: Don't be moved by others. Who cares whether they think we're wimps or not. We're not being patient if we're affected by what other people say. We must have our own guiding principles.

⊱⊰

Q: What is the relationship between the United States and the Middle East conflicts at this time?

A: U.S. may claim that it is administering justice, but it's actually afraid that it will lose its stakes. If it weren't for selfishness, they would be victorious anywhere with their military. It would not lose.

ชจด

Q: Why doesn't the Master call on high-ranking officials in the government?

A: The Precepts makes it clear that monastics should not visit politicians.

ชจด

Q: But their political ideologies are different.

A: Political ideologies are "owned by those who have virtue and lost by those who have no virtue."

ชจด

Q: Venerable Master, when you were in Northeast China, the Japanese invaded there. However, the Japanese, even today, refuse to admit that their behavior was invasive. Do you think they will repeat such moves?

A: They will eventually become extinct if they don't set a limit on their greed. If they haven't learned to change from past lessons such as their unconditional surrender after being hit by atom bombs, their future spells danger.

ᘒᘔᘓᘕ

Q: Our environment is being destroyed. If all the animals were to die, where will their spirits go to become reborn?

A: They will have immigrated to other countries! You don't believe it? Some Chinese like the United States, so they become American citizens. Some Americans like China, so they become reborn as Chinese. They don't need to naturalize to become Chinese citizens. Souls are the same. You ask me what evidence I have? The things I say now are evidence.

ᘒᘔᘓᘕ

Q: Planet earth currently faces major crises such as a polluted environment, corrupted officials, and other hopeless circumstances. Is there still hope and what methods can Buddhists employ to revert these situations?

A: Sever desire and love! Without them, everything will be okay. I don't care who disagrees; I have to say this nonetheless. It's up to you as to whether you believe it.

೫೧೫

Q: How come Buddhism doesn't encourage people to enjoy themselves?

A: "To suffer is to end suffering; to enjoy blessings is to end blessings." The money in the bank is always yours if you don't spend it. If you eat, drink, and be merry, then you will use up your saving very quickly.

೫೧೫

Q: Is the Western civilization on its decline?

A: That depends on what people do. If everyone does good things, then the fate of these countries will turn for the better. But if everyone does bad things, then the destiny of these countries will certainly be stricken.

ഇൻരു

Q: How do we prevent malicious people from violating us and cheating us?

A: Would you let wolves swallow you if they came to do that?

ഇൻരു

Q: Taiwan has a tradition for people not to save someone who is drowning. They call that person a "replacement," a "substitute for a ghost." By saving the person who is drowning, you get yourself in trouble. When another friend and I were in high school, we saved someone who was about to drown. According to Taiwanese customs, we had to eat noodles stewed with pigs' feet, food that is supposed to calm us. But we didn't eat any. Will we become sick or hurt because of that incident?

A: No. Nothing bad will happen to someone who tries to save people. Those customs and traditions are thought up by demons and ghosts. They are solutions concocted by fox spirits. They get passed around long enough that they became traditions. We have to save someone who's dying. How can we refuse to save someone who's dying?

Q: How can we save China?

A: Everyone should not smoke and not kill.

Student: After encountering the Buddhadharma, I have studied it quite seriously; but my friends and family still don't understand. They think that I have become too involved and tied down by demons. At this point, should I practice compassion and go with the flow, or should I grit my teeth and pull myself out of the sea of suffering that is birth and death? Please give me some instructions.

A: You have to be the unwavering candle in the windstorm, the enduring gold in the intense fire. You have to be undaunted to be a true disciple of the Buddha.

৪০০গ

Student: How does a non-Buddhist learn to bear pain from family and friends?

A: What kind of pain?

Student: Pain that comes when the man that you like doesn't reciprocate in kind.

A: Everything is a test to see what you will do, what I will do, and what he will do. If we don't recognize what is before us, we must start anew. We must truly recognize our faults in each difficult situation. Do not criticize others. If we really know our mistakes, we don't need to worry about whether other people are right or wrong. Others' faults are simply my own; knowing that we are all the same is great compassion. Be extremely kind to those with whom you have no affinities. Great compassion is to understand that we are all the same. By being kind and compassionate to people, we will have no more problems.

Q: Do you think it's better to yell at people or to bow to the Buddhas?

A: Sometimes it's good to yell at people too.

Q: Under what circumstance is it good to yell at people?

A: When mistakes are made.

Q: Mistakes made by whom?

A: By the one who gets yelled at.

&OG

Q: Why are there so many disasters in the world now? For instance, there are many more airplane crashes this year than last. What kind of retribution is this?

A: People get angry too often and kill too often!

&OG

Q: Will the Venerable Master explain from the Buddhist perspective why the Chinese never unite wherever they are, including in Malaysia?

A: They do this to help other people and other countries. It's negative in one respect and positive in another respect. For instance, we work during the day and rest at night, but if you think it's wrong to rest at night, then you will wear yourself out! They may be discordant and fragmented now, but when they have helped enough people, they will become united. That is how it will be. When things reach an extreme, they will turn around. When things become extremely negative, it will turn positive. Opposition is Tao's movement while weakness is Tao's function. If you can reverse your perspective and find the positives, then everything is OK. No problem.

ഓരു

Q: How can we save Taiwan?

A: Don't have abortions. Don't kill.

ഓരു

By Venerable Master: I would like to ask everyone, do people live to eat, or eat to live?

Disciple: We eat to live.

Venerable Master: Why do we live?

Disciple: For knowledge.

Venerable Master: What is knowledge for?

Disciple: To achieve our spiritual goals.

Venerable Master: That's right, we should all search for wisdom. With great wisdom, we will not be so confused. Why do we always act confused? It is because we don't have any wisdom. This is the fundamental issue. The Buddha realized Buddhahood for the sake of wisdom. We should do some meritorious things for the world, virtuous things for the citizens, and beneficial things for the entire human race. This is the duty of human beings, eating isn't it.

৪৩৫৪

Q: Is the consequence just as severe for people who have abortions because they don't have the financial means [for rearing a child] and other reasons?

A: Without the financial means, they shouldn't have gotten pregnant in the first place. They should have avoided the problem that would follow that act. Without the financial capabilities, why do they attempt to resolve problems only when they occur? Why do they have to wait until it's too late before they know that they're hungry and have to cook? They should have anticipated this when planning their yearly budget.

❧❦

Q: Some people mean well, but their actions actually result in harm. How should we deal with that?

A: If you try to help people in all respects, you will not cause people problems. If you try to help yourself in all respects, you will cause everyone problems.

❧❦

Q: The passage on the Ten Commandments in the Bible talks about how one of the commandments is related to being filial to one's parents. But Western culture for the most part has ignored this commandment. As for Buddhism, how can it claim that filial piety is the root of virtue since the Buddha left his parents?

A: Buddhism elevates filial piety so that it reaches its pinnacle. Most people think there's no filiality in Buddhism from what they see. The Buddha said, "Every man has been my father and every woman, my mother." He saw that all living beings are his parents from the past and are Buddhas of the future. Hence he is not toward any living being. He wants to save all living beings so that they become Buddhas. He has vows as terrific as that. That's why after he cultivated and realized Buddha-hood, he then came back to save all living beings so that they become Buddhas. This is filiality perfected. Every Buddhist Sutra talks about filiality. It's just that most people who don't understand the Buddhadharma see only the surface of the Buddha leaving home to cultivate, which to them meant that he didn't care about his parents. Actually, this is about wanting to be categorically filial to one's parents.

&ocs

Q: People are born, age, get sick, and die. Is it because of cause and effect that people become ill? Would people become free of illnesses if they were to do good deeds?

A: Not necessarily. For instance, some people want to have an abortion because they're afraid that the doctor would not earn enough money. The doctor [who performs abortions] must be intimately related to you, perhaps a relative or a friend of yours; otherwise, why would they be afraid that he would not get enough to eat?

&ocs

Q: How should we use our wisdom to do good deeds in our society now?

A: Wisdom means not being deluded.

&ocs

Q: If my friends take drugs, drink alcohol, and do bad things, how do I be kind and compassionate to them when they get angry?

A: Be careful about the kind of friends that you chose. Those who are near rouge become red, those who are near black ink become dark. Tainted by the color brown, one becomes brown; tainted by the color yellow, one becomes yellow. The best way to interact with a friend who does not meet one's own standards, that is, a bad friend, is to respectfully keep a distance.

ৡОС৪

Q: The society is divided into two different echelons: one is the wealthy while the other is the poor. The divide has become more and more obvious. The rich keep getting richer, while the poor get poorer. Essentially, we are already seeing the fire pyre down the road. How should we face this reality?

A: Put out that fire.

Q: Should someone who works in an occupation that is related to national defense switch jobs because they're actually indirectly killing people?

A: Wouldn't it be even better if you weren't born during this time in history? Wouldn't you have avoided all these problems? It would be good for you to change your occupation, but if you can't then you can recite the Buddha's name while you work. That way, national defense will be less effective in killing so many people.

Q: We respectfully request that the Venerable Master, out of compassion, pity the population of Taiwan who are lost in delusion and falseness, and come back to propagate the Buddhadharma every year so that the proper Dharma will live forever and thrive.

A: It's better that you come back than for me to come back. It's better if you quit running toward the outside.

৪০০৪

Q: What can we do to help someone who is lost and needs someone to help him set some goals?

A: Tell him so with utmost sincerity. Friends are people who are extremely sincere. Sincerity will move even stones so that they split open.

৪০০৪

Q: How can we accomplish great things?

A: Someone who can do great things will do what others cannot do. To be able to withstand the worst form of misery, one becomes the best among the best. But this is not about being different or competitive.

৪০০৪

Q: How can we bring peace to a country and its people?

A: The leaders of the country would have to be virtuous and at the same time be willing to employ worthy and capable individuals.

ৡৈওঙ

Q: What kind of attitude should we have when our family members do not get along?

A: The Vajra Sutra says, "All conditioned dharmas are like dreams, illusions, bubbles, and shadows, like dewdrops and flashes of lightning. We should thus contemplate."

ৡৈওঙ

Q: My first marriage was bad, and the second was worse. Why?

A: Then don't get married again. Recite Guan-shiyin Bodhisattva's name more often. become unified with mainland China?

ಬಂಣ

Q: Someone asked the Master to pray for blessings and quell disasters for the nations that are in chaos.

A: National leaders should be the ones to request the Dharma for quelling disasters for a nation. Dangerous situations will naturally be prevented and the country made secure if political officials don't accept bribes.

ಬಂಣ

Q: My husband wants to divorce me, but I don't want to. Will the Master please provide instructions?

A: Then be his friend.

ಬಂಣ

Q: What does "the world is in three divisions" in Great Master Bu Xu's predictions mean?

A: There will be three superpowers that lead

the entire world. "That's the world in three divisions."

∞∞

Q: My son and daughter-in-law are not very filial to me. Will the Master please provide some instructions for me?

A: You can quietly repent the karma that you had with them in the past. The causes from past lives become the effect of this lifetime. Recite Guanshiyin Bodhisattva's name often. Don't be resentful; the enmity can be resolved gradually.

∞∞

Q: Why do natural disasters occur?

A: The heads of states are not virtuous enough. Superiors and subordinates are all greedy.

∞∞

Q: My son wants to be the best in everything, what should I do?

A: Everyone wants to be first, so who will be second?

೮೦೮೩

Q: Since I've started to learn about Buddhism, I no longer enjoy social engagements. Many people say that I have become increasingly abnormal.

A: Isn't that to become normal?

೮೦೮೩

Q: Why do people gossip?

A: Because they're stupid.

೮೦೮೩

Q: How come my children never listen to me?

A: Because you treated your parents this way when you were young, too.

೮೦೮೩

Q: Will the Venerable Master please pick a lucky day and hour for the opening of my store?

A: Any hour is a good hour; any day is a good day.

ಬಂಚ

Q: My daughter is stubborn, ill-tempered, and disobedient.

A: Your daughter is just like you!

ಬಂಚ

Q: Master, I have fewer and fewer friends since I have begun studying Buddhism.

A: Why do you want friends?

ಬಂಚ

Q: My husband is having an affair; what should I do?

A: You've got a substitute ghost; you are now free!

Q: Will the Venerable Master please bless my son so that he doesn't become a bad person?

A: Parents should always discipline and teach their children.

Q: You say our body is like a toilet?

A: Every person's body is like a toilet. Our stomach houses feces and urine, for instance. So why do we love our body and value it so much? Our body is extremely filthy, so why do people consider it a gem, decorating it with diamonds, gold, silver, and jewelry or rubbing it with perfume and makeup? Aren't they decorating a toilet with flowers and jewelry?

Q: I am still young, but lots of girls call me. What should I do?

A: Tell them to study.

D
I
S
C
I
P
L
I
N
E

P
H
Y
S
I
C
A
L

B
O
D
Y

Q: What kind of causes and conditions bring people together?

A: The Avatamsaka Sutra says, "I have been a parent, a sibling, and a child to every living being since time immemorial..."

Q: Don't the rich suffer?

A: Yes. Their wealth could shrink and disappear. They may have lots of money and lots of property, but a fire could easily burn down their house and turn cash into ash. This is a form of suffering called decay. The wealthy experience the suffering of decay.

Q: I have been feeling miserable, too, since my daughter's divorce. What should I do?

A: You have to think of everyone in the world

S
U
F
F
E
R
I
N
G

O
F

T
H
I
N
G
S

G
O
I
N
G

B
A
D

as your children so that you will not be so miserable.

ఴౡ

Q: Why is the world in such mayhem that everything seems hopeless?

A: The world is in such a state of chaos and unrest because everyone is selfish and pursuing self-interests: "This is mine, that belongs to me." Cultivators must achieve the state of "no-self." What is there to fight for if there is no self? What is there to hanker after? What is there to be sought after? When we have settled our accounts, we figure out that we don't want a thing. We only want to learn to have the attitude of Bodhisattvas: sacrificing ourselves for the sake of others.

ఴౡ

Q: How can we become human beings [in the future]?

A: We will become human beings if we do good deeds. Check and see if we have done major or minor, many or few good deeds. Having done a lot of good deeds, we will become rich and belong to the upper class. Having done very few good deeds, we will become poor and belong to the lower class.

৪০৪৪

Q: My daughter has been in a lot of pain after her divorce.

A: The more she's in pain, the better.

৪০৪৪

*V*enerable Master: Does your mother-in-law want something?

*D*isciple: She wants to go out and buy a pair of shoes that fits her. I haven't had time to take her.

*V*enerable Master: Why don't you do it immediately?

Disciple: There are too many things to take care of in the temple.

Venerable Master: Don't be that way. Your mother-in-law's welfare comes first. Take care of temple business later. Don't leave her frustrated.

৪০ৎ৪

Q: Why is this world in such a mess?

A: Because the foundation upon which good human beings develop has not been built well.

৪০ৎ৪

Q: The retribution for the number of marriages one has had shows up after death. Depending on the number of times one has been married, one will be sawed apart by a large chainsaw that many times. What's so bad about being split apart from head to toe?

A: When you are split into several pieces,

your spirit will have a hard time regrouping. You may not have the human body again in billions and billions of eons. Your nature becomes transformed and your spirit disintegrated so that you are practically like a grass or tree, an insentient plant. It's difficult to become a sentient being once one has dismembered one's inherent nature.

ဆၢ

Q: What if my parents want me to do bad things?

A: See! Never having been filial and not having even taken the first step in filiality, you're already trying to circumvent it!

ဆၢ

Q: How do I make my husband believe in Buddhism?

A: Don't be so insistent!

ෆ**ෆ**

Q: We live in a polluted world, the water and land are polluted, the environment is polluted, and the air is polluted. Where did pollution come from?

A: It basically originated from our single thought of ignorance. The nature of ignorance is like fire: the bigger the fire, the more dark smoke looms over the world and pollutes families and human nature.

ෆ**ෆ**

A disciple's father passed away unexpectedly. The entire family was heartbroken, teary-eyed all the time.

Q: I want to see my father one more time, where is he?

A: It doesn't help to cry. You have to recite the Earth Store Sutra and dedicate merit that you generate by doing that to him. The more often you recite, the better.

*O*nce I brought my eldest daughter to Gold Wheel Monastery because I wanted the Venerable Master Hua to bless her so that she would find a good marriage partner.

The Venerable Master took a look at the daughter and with great kindness said: This child has a lot of affinities with Buddhism; unfortunately she is very emotional when it comes to relationships with the opposite sex. If she were to channel this kind of emotion into studying Buddhism or cultivating, she would be quite accomplished.

ৠৎ

Q: Many people are dissatisfied with the current state of social disorder. These people are all very educated and do not wish to comply with unscrupulous norms. As a result, they want to escape and come here to cultivate.

A: That kind of motive is faulty. They shouldn't be escaping reality; they should use what they've learned to save the human race and improve society.

৪০৫৪

Q: How can we make sure that there will be no Armageddon?

A: If we translate the Buddhadharma into English and other different languages, then people will stop being so apathetic. By making progress in their spiritual development, the world would be far removed from its end. Armageddon could be delayed until numerous great eons later, or, maybe the end of the world will never arrive. It's possible that the end of the world will not arrive because the great wheel of the Buddhadharma is being turned, for it magnetizes the sun in orbit so that it never disappears.

৪০৫৪

Q: How should parents admonish children who are not filial?

A: Parents should reflect, first of all. We should begin by being filial to our own parents. Action speaks louder than words. When children see that their parents are filial, they will naturally model after their parents and be filial. If you kick your parents out or speak to your parents harshly and with conceit, your children will naturally emulate you who are their role models. Behavioral lessons are vivid for children. Parents may talk all they want, but if they don't walk their talk, children will always feel that their parents are not filial.

ଽଔ

Q: Does reciting the Sutra really help him?

A: Yes! Just recite it sincerely and you will have your prayer answered.

ଽଔ

Q: What does Buddhism think of euthanasia? Is it completely forbidden?

A: The things that people do are neither absolutely and necessarily right nor absolutely and necessarily wrong. Not every legal prohibition is correct, necessarily. People may want to help the dying by killing them because they see that they are in pain. That is right in a sense. Buddhism forbids killing though; after all, this is about karma. It is karma that a patient suffers and should therefore face the consequences. We have no way to prevent someone from facing his karma.

৪৩৫৩

Q: Could patients who are vegetables try euthanasia?

A: I would be going against the universal principle of wanting to see things live if I were to approve of people trying euthanasia. At the same time, they probably would not be at peace or happy if their life continued. I can't answer this question.

ಬಂಐ

Q: What does Buddhism think of euthanasia (literally, "peaceful and happy death" in Chinese)?

A: What is euthanasia? How can death be peaceful and happy? We would only enjoy a peaceful and happy death if we were to have a certain level of cultivation from being mindful of the Buddha and can predict when we will be reborn in the Land of Ultimate Bliss. Buddhism has no opinion on euthanasia.

But if this kind of death is peaceful and happy, is it a peaceful and happy death for people who have committed suicide by hanging themselves, jumping into the river, and poisoning themselves? Is it so for those who have ended their lives voluntarily and willingly, despite others' efforts to prevent them from such acts?

I'm someone who doesn't know how to cultivate; I don't have the ability to teach you to die peacefully and happily. I have no way to teach you to live peacefully and happily either. I'm at my wits end when it comes to making you peaceful and happy as well as unpeaceful and unhappy. People are not the way they are because you want them that way. People do not stop their actions because you want them to avoid certain actions. This incredible process is called life.

ಹಾಡಿ

Q: How can we be filial?

A: By being compliant.

Education

Q: If the most important aspect of education is moral development, and if morality is our inherent wisdom, then isn't that concept the same as the Confucian idea that human nature is good?

A: You are inherently good if you don't do anything evil. If you do any evil, then, "Though our natures are similar, our habits are by far dissimilar."

ဆင်္ကြ

Q: "It is better to study nothing for a day than it is to study wisdom for a thousand days." What does this quote mean?

A: "Not knowing when to quit the studying of different terms, we only trap ourselves by counting sand in the sea." Who is learning wisdom for a thousand days? Who is learning nothing for a day? We should not keep on doing others' laundry.

ဆင်္ကြ

Q: What is the difference between learning one character a day and studying one character all day?

A: What is the difference between eating a meal and the meal which is being eaten?

೮೦೦೮

Q: How can we bring peace to our society?

A: We should start with education, teaching children to be filial to their parents and to be loyal to their country.

೮೦೦೮

Q: Can teachers go on strike?

A: Teachers can't go on strike. The pilots of an American airline went on strike once, and the public suffered. Educators should keep their conscience clean. Do the work of developing people for generations to come. If teachers readily go on strike, how can they be role models for students? How can they educate the next generation?

ಬಂಡಛ

Q: How should parents encourage their children to cultivate? Should they start cultivating at a young age or should they wait until a certain age before they begin to cultivate?

A: "We become red around rouge; we become dark around black ink." If you do what is good, then children learn that; if you do what is bad as parents, then children learn to be bad too. For instance, if the parents were to think about selling drugs all the time, the children would definitely smoke dope because they're too close to it.

ಬಂಡಛ

Q: The Buddhadharma encourages people to not fight or seek. Is it a form of fighting and seeking to want to be the best student or the most outstanding employee?

A: Live up to your responsibilities. In the reach of your intellectual capacity, you might as well read more books and do your assignments well.

⊷⊶

Q: I just want to learn more.

A: You have to empty your brain if you want to learn more. If you don't empty your brain and all that falsehood in it, you will not be able to put any Dharma in there.

⊷⊶

Q: You could just put it in my brain if you would.

A: You expect too much. When we build a house, we must lay the foundation well. Unless the foundation to the house is well-built, the house will not be solid. Of what use is a house with a collapsed foundation?

⊷⊶

Q: Now that I have taken the first step, what is the second step?

A: Take it slow. You don't even necessarily understand everything that I am saying right now. When you understand what I'm saying, then you will also understand why I don't say anything.

❧❧

Q: The youth that I teach don't listen to me. It's impossible to teach them. I have used everything. What are some methods can I use to make them listen? What kind of mantra should I recite?

A: Be patient, be patient, so po he.

❧❧

Q: I feel that I am really lazy. I find that many of my friends have the same problem. I often encourage them, as well as myself, to study, but I always feel that I have wasted too much time.

I struggle internally when I admonish them. If I can't even admonish myself to change, how can I admonish my friends?

A: Just study hard! There's an antidote to being lazy. This is not about reciting a mantra. To not be lazy, you have to become inspired. "The person who is committed will be successful." Let's not talk about being lazy. People who are committed and willful can achieve anything.

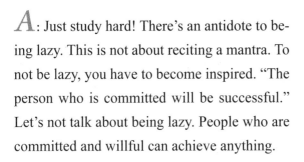

Q: I am a freshman at Berkeley. My parents are in Taiwan. Sometimes when I call home, I hear that Mom or Dad is sick or something. Yesterday, for instance, when I heard that my father was in the hospital for a surgery, I was in a very bad mood.

A: Just don't call. Don't worry about this and that when you are studying. Forget everything. Don't use your emotions. To call home is to use your emotions. They give you problems when they call you; you're not looking for problems. However, if you were to call them, then you would be looking for problems. Why can't you let go? You're the one who can't let go if you call home often. If you can let go, then even if there were problems, things would turn out fine. Don't be concerned. Just remember to be mindful of the Buddha.

ꔛꔛꔛ

Q: When I first heard about the Six Guiding Principles that the Master talks about, I thought they seemed difficult. They're hard to learn, especially true altruism. I believe that's very difficult. Does the Venerable Master have some class or school that we can attend, or some method to teach us to be unselfish?

A: Although people need to be taught this, they can begin with some small things, start from the beginning. If you teach kids how to be good people, how to interact with others, how not to compete to be the best and earn big bucks, then as selfless kids, they will not be crazy when they grow up. Some people say, "I can't learn that, I'm too old already." Some other people say, "I never learned it when I was young and I cannot learn it now. Now I just want to earn more money or get a promotion. I only know this much." Well, I still think people can change. Although the childhood of those in the prime of their life and those who are senior has long since passed, they can still retain the mentality of youth. You can start over with your actions. As it says, everything is a test to see what I will do, to see what you will do, to see what he will do. If you do not recognize the situation, you will have to start anew.

Q: What recommended antidote does the Venerable Master have for our bankrupted education?

A: The best medicine for education in this country is a wonderful prescription. It can solve the problems of every young person in the world, and that is: filiality and brotherhood. If teachers could behave as models and teach students to listen to their parents and to respect their teachers and elders from the start, then most of the dangers that we face now would never occur. The important thing is that if we don't know to teach young people the value of filiality, then any other things they learn will only take care of the symptoms and not the source. The prescription won't fit the illness. With regard to this issue, my proposed solution is that teachers should be role models and teach the foundation of every virtue--filiality.

ॐ

Q: May I ask the Venerable Master how a student in school now should study the Buddhadharma?

A: Students should focus on their school-work. You may try to soak up some Buddhadharma when you're not studying; but it would be wrong to focus only on the Buddhadharma and not your coursework. You must balance the two so that you don't overemphasize one aspect. Young people often make the mistake of neglecting their studies to study the Buddhadharma.

Q: Is it in accord with the Dharma for monastics to stand up and greet lay teachers for class?

A: It's okay with elder teachers. If you want to stand up, stand up. If you don't want to stand up, don't stand up. It's okay to sit and greet them with your palms together, too.

Q: I am a sophomore at the University of Berkeley. Recently, I feel a tremendous amount of pressure in studying. It's so competitive. I can't find a way to freedom and contentment. I wonder if there's any advantage to studying at this university. I don't know what to do.

A: Be calm and serene when you study. Don't think so much. Don't worry about what is good or bad and don't be concerned about loss and gain. Who gave you that pressure? You gave it to yourself. If you don't let the pressure get to you and just let things develop, then you will experience no pressure.

ନ୍ଦେୟ

Q: There are some duties that volunteer teachers at the schools are not able to do, is it okay to hire people for these things?

A: Yes, but the volunteer teachers are the bosses. The hired help has to listen to volunteer teachers.

ନ୍ଦେୟ

Q: Recently I read that a province in Canada is developing a curriculum on morality. However, I find that their content lacks some essentials. Although they discuss self-respect and self-love, they have basically forgotten that the most fundamental value: filiality to parents and respect for family values. My personal difficulty in teaching is that I have discovered that many young people live in harsh environments. Such as? Their families are broken; they may only live with their father or mother, or with their homosexual parents. So when I talk about being filial to parents, such youth have a hard time accepting this concept in their heart of hearts and difficulty applying it at home. Some parents even reject it when their children do their best to put it into practice at home. Will the Venerable Master and other instructors please tell me how teachers and elders can make a deep impression of the basic moral principles of filial piety and respect on the minds of children?

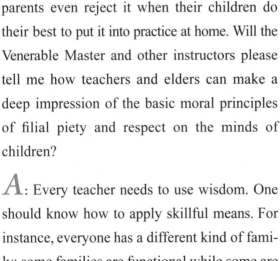

A: Every teacher needs to use wisdom. One should know how to apply skillful means. For instance, everyone has a different kind of family; some families are functional while some are dysfunctional. We cannot treat bad families the way we treat good families. This requires expedient means and compromises. Expedients must be applied appropriately. There is no fixed sequence to when and how an expedient is used. Everyone should come together to study these issues and apply effort to solve them with collective wisdom. These are not difficult issues. Filiality is for the average family. We have to use other means for families that are different and complex. There are typical methods and there are atypical - expedient - methods. The typical methods are more common while the expedient methods are skillful means for particular times and situations.

The Tao contains both the typical
and the expedient,
and they should both be used;
Phenomena separate into substance
and function,
and they should both be understood.

Comparison:
Buddhism & Others

Q: Please explain to me the relationship between Buddhism and Christianity.

A: They both teach you and me.

ॐ☙

Q: There are 84,000 Dharma doors. Are other religions such as Hinduism, Catholicism and Christianity considered Dharma doors?

A: Every dharma is the Buddhadharma, and none can be obtained.

ॐ☙

Q: What is the difference between prayer and Chan meditation?

A: If you think they're the same, then they are the same; and vice versa.

ॐ☙

Q: According to Buddhist scriptures, Lord Shakra of the Trayastrimsha Heaven is the same as the Jade Emperor that Taoists talk about. However, Taoists reject this parallel. Taoists say that the Jade Emperor and all Daluo Golden Immortals are outside the wheel of birth and death, therefore it's impossible for them to be in the Realm of Desire and to wage war against asuras. Will the Venerable Master please tell us the truth?

A: This issue is an unsettled lawsuit. An idiom goes, "An honorable judge can't settle family affairs." Well, this Dharma Master can't settle such religious affairs. Each religion claims that it is the best as it espouses its own principles. Actually, they're trying to scratch an itch on their foot through their boots. They're like the blind men who were feeling the elephant to figure out what it looked like. Do they know how tall, how big, and what color the Jade Emperor is? Do I know? Do you know? I believe there is no proof to any of this.

C
H
R
I
S
T
I
A
N
S

&

B
U
D
D
H
I
S
T
S

Q: Presently, Christians and Buddhists are having frequent discussions on their similarities and differences. They appear to be communicating and trying to understand each other. But I have a question: can a religion really accept another religion unconditionally? For example, can Catholics and Christians really believe that people will be saved through religions other than faith in the "one and only true God?"

A: I can't answer this question categorically as I have not attended the meetings with these religious leaders and they have not attended our meetings either. If you really want to know the truth, you should invite all the leaders of all the major religions around the world for a conference. They should sit down and speak directly, openly, and publicly about how they feel. Ask them if they can really accept each other wholeheartedly. If these religious people discriminate against others, praising themselves and condemning others, they would be violating the spirit of their founders. The purpose for the founding of every major religion was not to fight with other religions and not to insist that they alone are right while others are wrong.

Another important point to pay attention to: It is now trendy for Christians and Buddhists to organize seminars for frequent exchange of ideas. However, we must verify whether these so-called Buddhist organizations can really represent Buddhism. There are so many different kinds of pretenders in the West that we can't tell immediately if someone is legitimate, so we must observe them carefully. Not all who claim to be Buddhists really represent Buddhism. We should not be hoodwinked by them.

ಐಂಖ

Q: Master, what is the difference between Buddhism and theistic religions?

A: One is ultimate while the other is not.

ഇരൽ

Q: Christianity talks about how people join their family members in heaven after they die. What does Buddhism say about this?

A: Since they can reunite in heaven, how do you know they will not have a reunion in hell?

ഇരൽ

Q: What is the difference between Buddhism, Taoism and the Heavenly Way?

A: Buddhism is Buddhism; Taoism is Taoism; and the Heavenly Way is the Heavenly Way. Their names already indicate their difference.

ഇരൽ

Q: Are Taoism and Buddhism in the same family?

A: Are Chinese and Americans all human beings?

Q: What is the difference between Buddhism, Taoism, and Confucianism? Are they the same?

A: One represents elementary-level curriculum on morality; one represents secondary-level curriculum on morality; and one represents university-level curriculum on morality. The university curriculum tells you to take refuge with the Triple Jewel: the Buddha, Dharma, and Sangha. Don't forget the Triple Jewel. The secondary level curriculum tells you to take refuge with your essence, energy, and spirit. Don't expend them carelessly. Beginners are taught to perfect the ways of being human.

80C3

Q: Is Buddhism a theistic religion that talks about praying to god for miracles?

A: Buddhism is neither theistic nor non-theistic. It also isn't about praying for miracles or gains.

৪০৪৪

Q: Is there any difference between Taoism and Buddhism?

A: Taoism only goes halfway, whereas Buddhism takes it to the ultimate end. You don't really understand the Buddhadharma if you don't understand Taoism. You don't really understand Buddhism if you only understand Taoism. Taoism is only the beginning one or two steps; it only reaches the halfway mark.

৪০৪৪

Q: Is Confucianism's "disposing of objects and completing wisdom" different from Buddhism's disposing of objects?

A: Although they're different terms, they

mean the same. To "dispose of objects and complete wisdom" means that one should clear one's mind and lessen one's desires, which is to sever desire and love. Confucianism doesn't explain the disposing of objects the same way I do. It doesn't specify the object.

※※

Q: Where do Buddhism and Taoism differ?

A: Tell me the differences between old, middle-aged, and young people. Confucianism, Buddhism, and Taoism are in the same family, but respectively, one is a child, one is an adult in the prime of his life, and the other an old person. Would they understand the way each other think?

※※

Q: What is the difference between Buddhism and Catholicism? I don't understand this. Will the Venerable Master please explain?

A: What's the use of explaining this? You can believe in Catholicism if you prefer Catholicism. You reap what you sow. You can study Buddhism if that's what you like. It's a matter of preference for you. You reap the effect of the causes that you've sown. Whether they're similar or different, they're both about not doing any evil and doing everything that is good.

❧❧

Q: Are divinations done according to the eight trigrams effective?

A: Taoism, Confucianism, and Buddhism in China existed at the same time in China. Buddhism has endured and we have chosen to believe it because its teachings are ultimate. The teachings of Taoism and Confucianism are not ultimate. However, Confucianism and Taoism helped form a basis for belief in Buddhism. In fact, Lao Tzu of Taoism is an incarnation of Venerable Mahakasyapa of Buddhism and

Confucius is a transformed incarnation of the Youth of Water and Moon according to Buddhism.

ଉଦ୍ଓଃ

Q: Why there are no "wish sticks" at the City of Ten Thousand Buddhas?

A: Buddhism does not indicate asking spirits for predictions.

ଉଦ୍ଓଃ

Q: Confucianism talks about humaneness while Buddhism talks about compassion. There are numerous similarities between the two, please explain their differences and similarities to us.

A: To be extremely humane is to be compassionate. Compassion embodies humaneness. Humaneness is the seed of being a good person; it is the seed of goodness for practicing Buddhist precepts.

ഓരു

Q: Someone took a photograph of a great Dharma assembly hosted by someone who calls himself a Buddha. More than ten thousand people were in attendance. There are two white shadows in that photo; they are said to be two deceased individuals who came to be saved.

A: Someone who is virtuous does not need to organize any Dharma assembly and yet can still save thousands, tens of thousands, and count-less souls in the underworld.

ഓരു

Q: Master, how will the Panchen Lama's death affect Buddhism in China?

A: I will not respond to this question. I honestly don't know, so I absolutely will make no judgments and offer no criticisms on this. Although I don't have much to do after I have had my meal, I refuse to discuss this issue.

ಬಂಡ

Q: I have seen Buddhism fracture into numerous sects, is that right?

A: Every religion, including all phenomena and objects, exists because of living beings' karma and causes and conditions. Buddhism and other religions are not outside the principle of causes and conditions. As it is said, "Having penetrated one principle, one understands a hundred principles." Originally, religions were meant to restrict people's behavior and make them turn away from evil and turn toward good. However, when people become critical and exacting, sects and factions occur. Confrontations occur because of different sects and factions.

ಬಂಡ

Q: I would like Buddhism to be my faith, but my parents are Catholics. Am I being disrespectful to them by not following their faith?

How should I settle this dilemma?

A: Is it disrespectful to them for you to smoke dope? Is that a dilemma? I believe you don't smoke dope and that's why I'm answering you this way.

৪০০৪

Q: Now that the Venerable Master has shortened, even ended, the distance between the Mahayana and Theravada traditions, will you please also shorten the distance between Buddhism and Taoism and Confucianism?

A: Confucianism is for elementary school children. Taoism is for high school youth. Buddhism is for college students.

৪০০৪

Q: Why are both believers and non-believers of Buddhas all Buddhists?

A: Because no one is beyond [the principles of] Buddhism.

ಬಂಚ

Q: I have read many Buddhist books but they seem to be different from the Buddhism that the Venerable Master describes. The Tantric practices of the Secret School are completely different from anything that the Venerable Master says. May I ask what is the value of that kind of practice?

A: I am a lesser individual than the person who teaches that. If you want to listen to me, then listen to me. If you want to listen to him, then listen to him. I refuse to compare and say what is right and what is wrong. You choose for yourself. However, the Buddha never said that anyone can become a Buddha by having desires. The Shurangama Sutra says, "Without eliminating lust, one can not transcend defilements. It would be like steaming sand and hoping that it becomes rice."

ಬಂಚ

Q: I had a friend whose soul left his body when he was lying down. He even saw his body lying on the bed. What is going on there?

A: This type of situation occurs often. His soul leaves and then comes back. Cultivators must have the right type of knowledge and views. We don't need to pay attention to whether our soul leaves our body or not. Taoism describes how one has a midget that leaves one's body and then returns. Taoists such as Lyu Dongbin cultivated this type of primal immortality. It is not an ultimate route though. That's why he later took refuge with the Triple Jewel and requested Meditation Master Huang Long of the Song Dynasty to be his master.

৪৩৫৩

Q: I saw someone who calls himself an Unsurpassed Teacher but dresses like a layperson and uses Buddhism as an ad everywhere he goes.

A: He is a cult figure, not a real Buddhist.

ಬುಗ

Q: Will taking refuge [with Buddhism] add to the goodness of someone who is already following another religious tradition?

A: If I were to say that it would strengthen his roots of goodness, then that becomes an enticement. I refuse to answer that question.

ಬುಗ

Q: I would like to know if the coming of Maitreya Bodhisattva and Jesus are the same?

A: I'm not going to say when Jesus will come again. But it's still a long, long time before Maitreya Bodhisattva will come. Most people who don't really know claim that Maitreya Bodhisattva will come soon.

ಬುಗ

Q: Does Buddhism allow for geomancy?

A: Geomancy is in your mind. If your heart is in the right place, good spirits will naturally protect you.

ಬಂಡ

Q: How is enlightenment according to Buddhism different from the transformed nature that Good Samaritan Wang talked about?

A: The transformed nature is to transform the water that has frozen into ice back into water again. Enlightenment is neither water nor ice; everything is empty.

ಬಂಡ

Q: You spoke of Dharma Master Hsu Yun?

A: You've never heard of him, right? If you want to represent God Almighty and you don't even know Dharma Master Hsu Yun, then you have lots to learn.

Q: A Buddhist nun has been teaching a practice associated with Guanshiyin Bodhisattva recently. She stresses that we can become enlightened in one lifetime. May we ask the Venerable Master if we can become enlightened in one lifetime with the Proper Dharma?

A: Crazy.

※○※

Q: Why doesn't Buddhism include reading fortunes, prophesizing, and consulting geomancy?

A: Everything is made from the mind alone. Buddhism teaches people to seek wisdom, not to have so much that they're confused (double entendre: superstitious).

※○※

Q: Who is the god of wealth, the god of nobility and and god of joy [three gods in Chinese folklore]?

A: The god of wealth is by your side when you don't allow your essence, energy, and spirit to be lost. The god of nobility is next to you when you are noble enough to not lose your temper. Furthermore, you are in touch with the god of joy when you are happy.

I have a different theory from that of Chinese folklore. These three gods -- the god of joy, the god of nobility, the god of wealth -- are all right here inside us. However, we don't know how to find them. We run outside looking for them when they're essentially a part of us.

৪୦୯୫

Q: Master, is there a genesis or a source of creation for living beings? If living beings have existed since beginningless time, then is the number of living beings fixed? If they originate from somewhere, where might that be?

A: The genesis is "zero." Ask yourself where "zero" begins and ends? It has no beginning or end. If you break through "zero" so that it turns into "one," then there's a beginning. "One" comes from zero. Once there's one, then there's two, then three, four, five, six, seven, eight, nine, ten, and infinitely many numbers. How many living beings would you say there are in that case? If you twist "0" a bit, then it becomes the symbol for infinity.

The zero is also the symbol for yin and yang in Chinese philosophy. It's drawn differently in the West and in China. You have to cultivate so that you turn "1" into "0." You will then have returned to the source of creation. Do you understand the answer to your question now?

☙◊❧

Q: I am someone who has a mundane job. My question is, all the education and training that we receive through our lives are for developing our competitive spirit to win success. Everything else is just factors that help. But now we have suddenly found a new goal and can change from the course that we originally thought was correct. We must decide whether to take a fork or go down the middle of the road. Is this a dream? It is real? Or is it my imagination? May I ask another question? I would like to know if Brahmanism, which are what I am refering to as the fork in the road, and Buddhism, which I am referring to as the middle of the road, are in fact the same? Are they the same road with two different street names?

A: Having awakened enough to learn that we need not fight for fame and fortune, how could it be contradictory for us to no longer want to do so? How could that understanding be illusory or imagined? This principle is very simple; even young children can grasp it. For instance, if someone encounters a fire pyre on the road, should he proceed or turn around? Having walked to the end of the beach, should he jump in the sea of suffering or turn back? Is it a contradiction to turn around here? Is this not real? That is my response to your first question. As to your second question about whether Buddhism and Brahmanism the same, all the religions that I know of consist of people. If we evaluate from the point of view of human beings, then only the labels are changed, the substance is not. Whether or not people are American, Chinese, Japanese, Spanish, Mexican, German, French, they are called humans beings. Though they have different names, they are still people.

Q: The principles in Buddhism are more profound than any other religions', right?

A: There's no better or worse as far as religions go. Religions are just medicine to cure people's diseases. Once we have taken our medication and have recovered, why would we still need the medication?

Q: Do you have anything that you want to say to the followers of God Almighty?

A: God Almighty is an excellent name. Its mission is excellent too. It's very ambitious of you to want to readjust the relationship between human beings and God Almighty.

∞

Q: According to the Book of Matthew of the Christian Bible, the year 2000, there will be apocalypse and Judgment Day. Please let us know your view on this, Master.

A: Apocalypse could occur at any time; Judgment Day could occur at any time as well.

∞

Q: I'm a Jew. Judaism is excluded from the five major religions that the Venerable Master mentioned. I would like to know how Buddhism can cooperate with Judaism.

A: Judaism is Buddhism. Catholicism is

Buddhism. The labels to these medicines have changed, but not the medicines themselves. These terms may change, but their definitions do not. I don't consider any religion a religion. Different religions simply represent the changes in human nature. So I belong to whatever religion I see.

୨୦୦୪

Q: Why do I always meet up with fortunetellers?

A: Because they want to come and test you in person. They are trying to find out how fond you still are of money. They want to see if they can entice you to get involved in get-rich-quick schemes. They want to check and see if you have any samadhi. "Everything is a test to see what you will do. If you do not pass the test, you must start anew."

୨୦୦୪

Q: Recently, I heard people say, "People should first become enlightened and then cultivate seriously." Some say, "If you come to me, you will become enlightened as soon as I give you my blessings. Then you can go on to really cultivate.'" When I heard this, I thought it was very strange because we have always known that we have to cultivate first before we can become enlightened and be certified to the fruition. I would like the Venerable Master to please explain this seemingly contrary theory.

A: This is too esoteric. I only understand principles that are ordinary; I don't understand principles that are too esoteric.

ৠᑕᑫ

Q: My older sister is close to a deviant sect that cheats others by claiming to be the Dharma Protector of Earth Store Bodhisattva. How can I convince her to stay away from them?

A: She will turn around after you understand yourself.

๛ඏ

Q: My family used to worship Matzu (Goddess of the Sea) at home. Since we started learning about Buddhism, we have been worshiping the Buddhas. Please let us know if we can make offerings to Matzu along with the Three Sages?

A: If you want to, you can make offerings to all the Sanghas and Buddhas throughout space. Buddhas are not competitive .

๛ඏ

Q: Many people are puzzled because a certain female has so many disciples. We hope to gain a better understanding by attending this Dharma Assembly so that we can prevent these disciples from walking down the wrong path.

A: When you took refuge with the Triple Jewel, the text to taking refuge made it very clear: "I would rather give up my life than to take refuge with demons and heretics ever."

❧❀❧

Q: My parents believe in Mazu (Sea Goddess), the Holy Mother of Heaven. We also have the three sages of the West on our altar. Is it okay for me to bow to all simulutaneously?

A: Cultivators must be kind and humble, being respectful toward everything. All living beings have the Buddha nature; all are capable of becoming Buddhas, even mosquitoes and ants. It would be more than enough if they turn away from confusion and return to enlightenment. There's no need to differentiate.

❧❀❧

Q: Who are those of the "outside Way" (non-Buddhists)?

A: They look for answers outside their minds.

ಬಂಚ

Q: What is your religion?

A: My religion concerns truth: with regard to human beings, to sentient creatures, to all that is mundane, and to transcendental wisdom.

ಬಂಚ

Q: What is the "S"-like line that separates yin from yang in the symbol for taiji?

A: Nothing. It's yang if we're attached to yang. It's yin if we're attached to yin. When we do not have either of those attachments, it doesn't belong to either side, for in and of itself, it is nothing.

ಬಂಚ

Q: Master, what kind of Bodhisattva is the Great Immortal Huang in Hong Kong?

A: The Great Immortal Huang in Hong Kong is just an immortal, but a very efficacious one. He saves ignorant people who don't understand principles that are profound and deep, so only superficial little magic tricks can be used with them! That way they will develop faith.

Q: Many faiths do not believe in reincarnation. Do you have any way to resolve that?

A: You may talk to elementary school kids about high school courses but they will not understand. You may talk to high school kids about college courses, but they will not understand either. Whether they believe reincarnation or not is just a matter of time. We don't need to be concerned about these issues needlessly.

৪৩০৪

Q: Why don't disciples of a certain non-Buddhist sect study the Shurangama Sutra?

A: The Shurangama Sutra is a mirror that

reflects demons. The demon-reflecting mirror makes their true character appear.

ഇൻരു

Q: Today I saw some really awesome people. One made recitation beads smell pleasant, and another person grew his arm so that it was really long!

A: Can these things make someone become liberated from the cycle of birth and death? What is a long arm good for?

ഇൻരു

Q: Then why are there books about qigong?

A: Those books contain only general descriptions by writers who have limited understanding of the excesses in qigong. They even get some terms mixed up so that the labels don't fit their content. For instance, the term 'martial arts for energy' is not an accurate description of what qigong is. At its extreme, qigong is a form of controlling others and is governed by demons. When qigong is used in this way, practitioners enter demonic states. We might term it 'a martial arts for ghosts' because when applied in this way, practitioners are possessed by ghosts and made to shake and tremble. One well-known qigong master described this as being, 'a martial arts that is self-initiated.' Most people have no idea what that means. When a practitioner begins to shake, it is because a ghost has been able to take possession of that person due to his or her lack of samadhi power. Most people don't understand what is happening and are convinced that this so-called martial arts is an internal practice. Little do they know that people who use qigong as a 'martial arts of ghosts' are able to command external entities to possess practitioners. If a practitioner has samadhi power, then unders such circumstances, he or she will remain calm and will not shake and tremble.

An illustration of this is the extending of an arm, which was mentioned perviously. It's not the person's own energy that compels the arm to extend. Rather, it is an external entity that has possessed the person's mind and thus is causeing the arm to extend. People in China are cautious about discussing things like spirits, ghosts, and monsters, and so most do not know that they are practicing 'a martial arts for ghosts.' Qigong has become a catch-all the name for a whole range of practices.

Qi has no sense of awareness and cannot function on its own, so how can it be a martial art? It scatters as soon as it leaves our body. Most people don't know about this and call it qigong, qigong. They may die from such misconceptions about qi, but they're still into their martial arts.

ଚୈଓଃ

Q: That qigong master is well-known in China, but he is not necessarily the best master. There are masters who are even more excelled in this art but have not yet made themselves known.

A: He said his teacher is several thousand years old. I say my disciple is several thousand years old. This is true.

സാരു

Q: Master, can you help prevent these extremes in qigong?

A: The ghosts see me and run away.

സാരു

Q: This well-known qigong master is a vegetarian, isn't that a form of cultivation on his part?

A: He eats witchcraft.

സാരു

Q: Someone claims he can
can show people a way to get rich.

A: I'm afraid that before you get rich, he will
have already swindled everyone's money and
become rich himself.

ဆာ၄သ

Q: Why are there so many cults and heretics
nowadays?

A: Those who are true are
afraid of being known;
those who are false
want others to know.

Q & A - Comparison

The Dharma Realm Buddhist Association

The Dharma Realm Buddhist Association (DRBA) was founded by the Venerable Master Hsuan Hua in the United States of America in 1959 to bring the genuine teachings of the Buddha to the entire world. Its goals are to propagate the Proper Dharma, to translate the Mahayana Buddhist scriptures into the world's languages and to promote ethics in and

Great and small vanish;
    internal and external dissolve.
Pervade every mote of dust;
    encompass the Dharma Realm!
All interpenetrates, meshing perfectly;
    interrelationships are unhindered.
With two clenched fists,
    shatter the covering of space.
In one mouthful,
    swallow the source of lands and seas.
With great compassion rescue all,
    sparing no blood or sweat.
    Never pause to rest!

Understanding the principles, we apply them
in specific matters.

We carry on the single pulse of the patriarchs'
mind-transmission.

During the five decades since its inception, DRBA has expanded to include international Buddhist centers such as Gold Mountain Monastery, the City of Ten Thousand Buddhas (CTTB), City of the Dharma Realm (CDR) and various other branch facilities. All these facilities operate under the guidance of the Venerable Master and through the auspices of the Dharma Realm Buddhist Association. Following the Buddhas' guidelines, the Sangha members in the DRBA monastic communities maintain the practices of taking only one meal a day and of always wearing their precept sashes. Reciting the Buddha's name, studying the teachings, and practicing meditation, they dwell together in harmony and personally put into practice the Buddha's teachings. In accord with Master Hua's emphasis on translation and education, the Association sponsors translation and publication centers where members of the Buddhist Text Translation Society carry out their work as volunteers. Educational opportunities include Sangha and Laity vocational training programs at CTTB and CDR, Dharma Realm Buddhist University programs at CTTB and in Berkeley, and elementary schools and accredited secondary schools programs at CTTB. The Association also conducts volunteer programs that cover a range of religious services. Buddhist Sunday school programs function at most of the Association's 30-some branches in the Americas and Asia.

This Association is open to sincere individuals of all races, religions, and nationalities. All who are willing to put forth his/her best effort in nurturing humaneness, righteousness, merit and virtue in order to understand the mind and see the nature are welcome to join in the study and practice.

White Universe

Ice fills the sky; snow covers the ground.
Countless tiny creatures perish in the cold
or sleep in hibernation.
While in stillness, contemplate;
*   in the midst of movement, investigate.*
Dragons spar and tigers wrestle
*   in continual playful sport;*
Ghosts cry and spirits wail,
*   their illusory transformations strange.*
Ultimate truth defies description;
*   it cannot be conceived of or expressed.*
*   Advance with haste!*

Great and small vanish;
  internal and external dissolve.
Pervade every mote of dust;
  encompass the Dharma Realm!
All interpenetrates, meshing perfectly;
  interrelationships are unhindered.
With two clenched fists,
  shatter the covering of space.
In one mouthful,
  swallow the source of lands and seas.
With great compassion rescue all,
  sparing no blood or sweat.
  Never pause to rest!

Dharma Realm Buddhist Association
The City of Ten Thousand Buddhas

4951 Bodhi Way, Ukiah, CA95482 U.S.A.

Tel: (707) 462-0939   Fax: (707) 462-0949

Home Page: http://www.drba.org

E-mail: cttb@drba.org

The International Translation Institute

1777 Murchison Drive,

Burlingame, CA 94010-4504 U.S.A.

Tel: (650) 692-5912   Fax: (650) 692-5056

Institute for World Religions
(Berkeley Buddhist Monastery)

2304 McKinley Avenue, Berkeley, CA 94703 U.S.A.

Tel: (510) 848-3440   Fax: (510) 548-4551

Gold Mountain Monastery

800 Sacramento Street, San Francisco, CA 94108 U.S.A.

Tel: (415) 421-6117   Fax: (415) 788-6001

Gold Sage Monastery

11455 Clayton Road, San Jose, CA 95127 U.S.A.

Tel: (408) 923-7243   Fax: (408) 923-1064

The City of the Dharma Realm
1029 West Capitol Ave.,
West Sacramento, CA 95691 U.S.A.
Tel: (916) 374-8268   Fax: (916) 374-8234

Gold Wheel Monastery
235 North Avenue 58,
Los Angeles, CA 90042 U.S.A.
Tel: (323) 258-6668   Fax: (323) 258-3619

Long Beach Monastery
3361 East Ocean Boulevard,
Long Beach, CA 90803 U.S.A.
Tel: (562) 438-8902   Fax: (562) 438-8902

Blessings, Prosperity, and Longevity Monastery
4140 Long Beach Boulevard,
Long Beach, CA 90807 U.S.A.
Tel: (562) 595-4966   Fax: (562) 595-4966

Avatamsaka Vihara
9601 Seven Locks Road,
Bethesda, MD 20817-9997 U.S.A.
Tel/Fax: (301) 469-8300

Gold Summit Monastery
233 First Avenue West,
Seattle, WA 98119 U.S.A.
Tel: (206) 284-6690   Fax: (206) 284-6918

Gold Buddha Monastery
248 East 11th Avenue,
Vancouver, B.C. V5T 2C3 Canada
Tel: (604) 709-0248   Fax: (604) 684-3754

Avatamsaka Monastery
1009-4th Avenue, S.W.
Calgary, AB T2P 0K8 Canada
Tel: (403) 234-0644   Fax: (403) 263-0637

Dharma Realm Buddhist Books Distribution Society
11th Floor, No. 85, Sec. 6, Jhongsiao E. Rd.,
Taipei, Taiwan
Tel: (02) 2786-3022   Fax: (02) 2786-2674

Dharma Realm Sagely Monastery
No. 20, Dong-Si-Shan-Jhuang., Singlong Village,
Liouguei Township, Kaohsiung County, Taiwan
Tel: (07) 689-3713   Fax: (07) 689-3870

Amitabha Monastery
No. 7, Sih-jian-huei, Chihnan Village,
Shoufong Township, Hualien County, Taiwan
Tel: (03) 865-1956   Fax: (03) 865-3426

Dharma Realm Guanyin Sagely Monastery
161, Jalan Ampang, 50450 Kuala Lumpur, Malaysia.
Tel: (03) 2164-8055 Fax: (03) 2163-7118

Prajna Guanyin Sagely Monastery
Batu 5 1/2 Jalan Sungai Besi, Salak Selatan,
57100 Kuala Lumpur, West Malaysia
Tel: (03) 7982-6560 Fax: (03) 7980-1272

Lotus Vihara
136, Jalan Sekolah, 45600 Batang Berjuntai,
Selangor Darul Ehsan, Malaysia
Tel: (03) 3271-9439

**Malaysia Dharma Realm Buddhist Association
Penang Branch**
32-32C, Jalan Tan Sri Teh Ewe Lim,
11600 Jelutong, Penang, Malaysia
Tel: (04) 281-7728 Fax: (04) 281-7798

Fa Yuan Sagely Monastery

1, Jalan Utama, Taman Serdang Raya,
43300 Seri Kembangan, Selangor, Malaysia
Tel: (03) 8948-5688

Source of Dharma Realm

Lot S130, 2nd Floor, Green Zone, Sungai Wang Plaza,
Jalan Bukit Bintang, 55100 Kuala Lumpur, Malaysia
Tel: (03) 2164-9055

Guan Yin Sagely Monastery

No. 166A Jalan Temiang,
70200 Seremban, Negeri Sembilan, Malaysia
Tel/Fax: (06) 761-1988

Buddhist Lecture Hall

31 Wong Nei Chong Road, Top Floor,
Happy Valley, Hong Kong, China
Tel: (852) 2572-7644   Fax: (852) 2572-2580

Gold Coast Dharma Realm

106 Bonogin Road, Mudgeeraba
Queensland 4213 Australia
Tel: (61) 755-228-788   Fax: (61) 755-227-822